STORIES OF A WEST VIRGINIA FAMILY

Greenbrier Almond
K Almond
Anne Almond
Ruthie Almond Wiewiora
Beth Almond Ford

International Standard Book Number 0-87012-861-2
Library of Congress Control Number 2015917268
Printed in the United States of America

Copyright © 2015 by
Greenbrier Almond
K Almond
Anne Almond
Ruthie Almond Wiewiora
Beth Almond Ford
Buckhannon, West Virginia
All Rights Reserved
2015

McClain Printing Company
Parsons, WV
www.mcclainprinting.com
2015

Front cover photo by Lois Flanagan Almond

DEDICATION

We dedicate these stories to our Mom and Dad
who gave us the gift of words and the freedom to grow.

CONTENTS

FOREWORD	vii
THANKS	viii
INTRODUCTION	ix
MOM'S JOURNAL	xi

GOING ON A CALL — 1
- YOU WILL NEVER FORGET — 2
- COUNTRY LIVING — 5
- WORKING AT DAD'S OFFICE — 6
- CHRISTMAS HOUSE CALL — 9
- OLD IRONSIDES — 10

MOM — 13
- MOM WAS SAFE — 14
- FIGURING OUT MOM — 15
- MOTHER MINE — 17
- KIND TO A FAULT — 20
- MY MOTHER-OF-PEARL — 22

FIRST DAY OF SUMMER — 25
- THE WHOLE SUMMER AHEAD — 26
- COME OUT AND FEEL THE WORLD — 28
- SUMMER PLEASURES — 30
- SUMMER OF '71 — 32
- SUMMER PLANS — 34

A WALK REMEMBERED — 37
- HOME AGAIN. HOME AGAIN. — 38
- GOOD FOR WHAT AILS YOU — 40
- WALK ON, MY CHILDREN — 43
- FRIENDSHIP LANE — 45

TAKING A WALK IN GRANDMA'S GARDEN	48
MAIN STREET	**51**
OUR LITTLE CORNER OF THE WORLD	52
WE WHO RULED	54
STORES TO VISIT	56
SATURDAYS ON MAIN STREET	57
OUR TOWN	59
THE ROLE OF SPIRITUALITY	**63**
YIN YANG CHRISTIANITY	64
THEOLOGY OF GRACE	66
SPIRITUAL TRUTHS	68
A FIRM FOUNDATION	70
GRANDDAD, THE PREACHER MAN	72
MY SIBLING	**75**
SISTER BETH	76
BIG BROTHER GREENBRIER	77
MY LITTLE SISTER RUTH	80
ANNIE	82
SISTER K	84
WEST VIRGINIA	**87**
WEST VIRGINIAN—THAT'S WHO I AM	88
MY HOME IN THE HILLS	90
"MOUNTAINEERS ARE ALWAYS FREE"	92
THREE DEGREES OF SEPARATION	94
WEST VIRGINIA INSIDE	96
MISCELLANY	**99**
BOOK BINDING	100
FOUR-LEAF CLOVER	102
HOPPING DOWN THE BUNNY TRAIL	103
WHERE THE RHODODENDRONS GROW	105

UPON MY WORD	108
WHAT I MISS MOST ABOUT CHILDHOOD	110
HEY DAD!	111
LIKE A TREE	114
REALLY SICK	116
P-NEUMONIA	119
SIXTH GRADE JITTERS	121
MY BRIER	123
EASTER	126
OPEN BOOK	127
4-H CAMP	128
A SECURE PLACE	130
HE FELL OUT OF BED AND CHANGED OUR LIVES	132
MOTHERS OF BUCKHANNON	135
UNITED NATIONS ON THE HILL	138
ALSO AVAILABLE	140

FOREWORD

Harold Almond and I became students together at West Virginia Wesleyan college in 1938 and have been friends ever since. Our future wives, Lois and Sarah, joined us in 1939. We all returned to Buckhannon in 1949 having finished a few years of military service, and our lives were closely entwined even more.

Back then house calls were routine and often to the far ends of the county and beyond. Harold often went to Pickens and I think he enjoyed doing so. He savored the fact that with his Jeep, no site was unreachable. I had the sense that he thrived on adversity.

I personally am very happy that I came back to Buckhannon and Upshur County with its natural beauty and wonderful, friendly people. I know Harold shared the same sentiments as I. The great thing about being a family doctor is that you treat all ages and often several generations of the same family. These patients often become good friends and even seem like family.

Our children, the Chamberlain Five and the Almond Five, grew up here and were friends. My wife Sarah became very close to Lois. Sarah admired and loved Lois very much. The Almonds were the epitome of a close-knit, caring family.

Harold always had an interesting way of expressing himself, starting back in college when he and Lois had a regular column in the Wesleyan *Pharos*, and he later was a regular contributor to the *West Virginia Hillbilly*, published for years by Jim Comstock of Richwood. Lois was also a writer, especially stories for her grandchildren.

It is a joy to see that their five children seemingly inherited their parents' skill as writers. Read on!

Blessings,
Dr. Robert Chamberlain

THANKS

We thank our Mom and Dad, who gave us the gifts of life, words, curiosity, and a love for each other. We thank our families, who kept the home fires burning as we met for writing retreats. And we thank Kimberly Gilmore for her conscientious editing and her patience with each of us and our strong-headedness. We especially want to thank the folks of Upshur County, West Virginia, both in our growing up years and now.

INTRODUCTION

It has always been a dream for the Almond siblings to put their stories on paper. I think we've all been asked to "write a book" and not let the tales of our West Virginia childhood disappear. It took years and the birth of grandchildren and great-nieces to finally spur us onto the task. I am the youngest of the siblings and, at least growing up, often found myself being the recipient of advice from the elders. The reverse was true with this book. I teach memoir writing classes and workshops, using a favored method of giving the students a topic and letting them write in a flowing and unencumbered manner, simply getting the story out and on the page. Over the course of several years, meeting in our various homes in West Virginia, North Carolina, Florida, and Virginia, we came up with these stories. Some came easily, some with blood, sweat, and tears. We grew stronger as a family and our love blossomed. We hope other families might be persuaded to undertake the challenge. It is a gift.

Beth Almond Ford

MOM'S JOURNAL

Our mother was amazing. She actually wrote things down. Like this, in 1954, when she had four of her five children.

From Mom's journal:

> I would like to share with you some of the happiness I have gleaned from my constant companionship with our four youngsters. Our little boy, Greenbrier, is 5½ and is starting to school next year. K is 4½ and is very serious and interested in learning as much as she can about everything. Anne is a lovable 3-year-old and just bubbling over with kindness and generosity. Our baby Ruth is not yet a year old and is, of course, the pet of the family.
>
> They talk back and forth about many things and I overheard K telling Anne about "My friend up in Heaven named God." I was consoling her after a reprimand by telling her how much I loved her, and she answered, "Yes, and Jesus loves me too."
>
> Children have their little spats, of course, but on the whole, they are really little peacemakers. Not so long ago, Anne and K were having trouble at the breakfast table—crying and shouting—and Greenbrier said, "I might tell a joke—and that would make the fight go out."
>
> Several weeks ago, our minister preached a sermon called "Taking Inventory of Ourselves," and I remarked at the dinner table afterwards that the sermon had been hard on me. Greenbrier immediately suggested a solution: "You'd better stay home next time, Mother."
>
> Last month on an especially beautiful morning, K stepped out of doors into the lovely fresh air and sunshine and exclaimed, "Oh Greenbrier, come out and feel the world."
>
> And I remember last summer. "Glory, Mama, I've got

Glory!" My chubby little sparkly-eyed 3-year-old Annie came running into the house with her hands full of blue flowers. Her daddy had held her high on his broad shoulders where she could reach the Heavenly Blue Morning Glories. She picked the delicate blossoms, and it was at this point that she came to share them with her mother.

How easy, with hardly any effort at all she had all the glory she needed—and all the peace and good will. How childlike—and yet, what a beautiful lesson she taught me.

Glory. Glory. Glory.

GOING ON A CALL

YOU WILL NEVER FORGET
Beth

"Come on, Bethie. Hop in, Happy. We've got a sick man out Sago way." Dad grabbed his black bag and we jumped into the Jeep, Happy curling his collie body into a circle on the back seat. With a grinding of the gears, Dad backed out of the driveway, giving a wave to Mom standing in her usual send-off spot at the front door.

Dad could be talkative if I got him telling me a story, but today he looked pensive and thoughtful. He remained quiet as we navigated the streets in town and headed south on WV Route 20, a twisty two-lane road. Sometimes we drove this way if we were going to the Game Farm, and I thought about a house call a few weeks ago. The old lady there had given me ammonia sugar cookies, soft and crumbly with a hint of lemon and something else.

Dad slowed the Jeep when we got to the miniature church and made the left onto the Sago-Hampton Road. "Bethie, this one might be a bit rough, honey. I don't want you to eat anything if they offer it—just 'no thank you' and leave it at that. I imagine we'll be about ready to stop for a popsicle when we finish up. You understand, Sugar?" I nodded my head and looked out the window as we turned again, this time onto a dirt road.

Dad sounded more serious than usual and I asked, "Is someone going to die? Maybe I should stay in the Jeep."

Dad glanced over at me, "Bethie, I'm going to need your assistance. This is a family with lots of children. Hell, there's chickens and children everywhere, but their father is seriously sick. Black lung and he's about coughed out all the lungs he has left." At this point Dad started into something about pneumococci and I started fretting about what I was going to say to all those children. Sometimes I wondered if Dad remembered I was his kid who was in kindergarten. With five children, he sometimes mixed us up. Or so it seemed to me. Especially at times like this.

We drove deeper into the woods, crossed through a creek, and I was brooding on my misgivings for not staying home and watching *As the World Turns* with Mom, when we started bouncing on a path up the steep side of a mountain. The Jeep engine was roaring and I grabbed hold of Happy's neck to keep us both from bouncing out the window. We came up and over the top onto a flat, barren, cinder-covered field with a shack on one side and a tiny cave across the way, an opening into a small family-sized coal mine. Two dogs came out from behind an abandoned car on blocks, pacing and snarling when Dad turned the engine off. Happy, surely a sainted dog, calmly stood up in the seat and turned his long nose at first one pup and then the other one. He looked over at Dad and seemed to nod his head, conveying the message "all clear." Grabbing his bag, Dad opened his door, and we all hopped out.

A tall thin woman, probably in her early 40's but looking 60, stood in the cock-eyed doorway of their tar papered shack. Children of all sizes peeked out behind her long skirt, eyes big, mouths closed, as they watched the doctor come striding toward the house. I stumbled and blushed, but the children's focus was on the collie who made his way straight to the woman and tilted his face up to her eyes and then playfully nuzzled the youngest child, standing upright, hanging on to his mother's apron. He giggled and the other children crept around their mother, wrapping their arms around Happy's neck. I think I realized then the wisdom of my father and his gentle approach to his patients through the love of a dog.

"Thank heavens you found us, Doc," the woman said. "It's James and he's hurting something awful, can't hardly catch his breath. Come on inside."

The coal smoke was thick and my eyes watered. Their entire house was one room, hardly any bigger than our kitchen. The children shyly smiled at me and pointed to their sagging couch. Across the room, back in a dark corner, a man moaned. Dad went over to him, pulling on a string over the small bed, illuminating the area with a naked light bulb on the ceiling. The children looked down at the dirty floor. I took a deep breath and tried not to gag. Unwashed bodies, coal dust, the odor of sickness, ramps cooking on the black stove—it was all so overwhelming. I would not be sick. I would make Daddy proud. I started asking the names of the kids, who were obviously scared and worried about their father.

Talking softly to the man, Dad gave him a shot and his pains and groans subsided. After grasping the woman's hand and shaking his head at her worried comment about payment, Dad and I took our leave. Climbing into the Jeep, Happy gave me a reassuring nuzzle and took his spot in the back. We headed over the slag-filled lane and I asked, "Daddy, why did everything have that bad odor?"

"Bethie," he said, "you'll never forget it the rest of your life, no matter where you are in the world. That, Sugar Plum, is the stench of poverty."

COUNTRY LIVING
Ruthie

We had gone miles and miles in Daddy's Jeep, deep into the wilds of Upshur County. The two-lane road had turned into gravel, and now into a grassy lane.

I hopped out, as Dad directed, to open the gate that kept the cows in. The metal gate was heavy for a little 5-year-old girl, but I was helping Dad and put all my energy into shoving it open. The Jeep pulled through the opening; I pushed the gate shut and climbed back into my seat.

Down, down, down the lane we rolled past trees and trees, then blackberry bushes, and out into the pasture area. We drove across a tiny stream and up to the side of a farmhouse. The old couple there welcomed us. As Daddy saw to the needs of his patient, the old lady led me into her kitchen. Would I like a drink of water? Yes, please. She drew the bucket up from the porch well, dipped out a dipper of cold water and handed me a glassful. The hour's drive had made me thirsty, and the cold water tasted fresh. Their home was cozy and self-sufficient. They had almost everything they needed down in that valley.

After giving some medicine and instructions to the wife, Dad asked about their garden. It was growing nicely out by the side of the house. What about the blackberries? The old man said they would be ripe in about a week and he should be well enough to pick some by then. Would Doc like some? Dad ordered a few quarts that the couple's neighbor would deliver into town about mid-month. That would be an even exchange for the house call.

Before we left, I needed to pee. The old woman showed me the outhouse, which was clean, lye-dusted, and spider-free. I had used these holes in the ground before. I was always a little afraid I might fall in. However, the job got done. I washed my hands in the basin out by the steps. Dad and I headed back toward town. The next morning would find me back at my kindergarten table with another adventure to share with Brent, Mike and Steve. Memories of that early fall afternoon would come again when our family ate blackberry pie for dessert after supper a few weeks later.

WORKING AT DAD'S OFFICE
Anne

Lightheaded and sweaty, I focused on my assigned task to cut the black thread after Dad expertly looped each small stitch. Our brave young patient, a nine-year-old girl who had cut her leg pretty badly, must not notice my anxiety. Just as the room started spinning, Dad said, "Thanks, Anne. Six stitches should be enough. Good job." Taking a deep breath, I rushed out of the exam room, thankful I had not fainted. I was determined my father would not know my secret. As much as I adored him, I could never become a nurse.

About twice a year, Dad would ask K and me if we were available to work in his office when his nurses took their vacations. While we knew Dad had an ulterior motive—he wanted his four daughters to become nurses—we liked to spend time with Dad and he paid us generously so, naturally, we said yes.

Dad's office was an interesting place to work. The building itself was a simple, sturdy little red brick structure on Kanawha Street that Uncle Walter built in 1957. Its 1200 square feet included a large patient waiting room with knotty-pine paneling, faux leather couches, a green linoleum floor, and *Life, Highlights,* and *Ebony* magazines. Tucked in the back were two exam rooms, a small nurse's office, a teeny bathroom, and a lab area. Everything had its place and each nook served a double function. Patient files and pharmaceutical samples crowded the nurses' area. Dad's desk sat in the larger exam room. A refrigerator for medicines, floor scales, and an all-important box of lollipops squeezed into the lab area along with Dad's essential coffee pot. Even the hallway served two purposes—it was exactly 20 feet between the back entrance and the wall where the eye chart hung. Undoubtedly, Mom and Dad had huddled together many hours to design the functionality of each space and to plan this little office with care.

Simple looks aside, the office hummed with noise and activity during the well-established hours of Monday through Saturday 9 a.m.-1 p.m. and Monday, Wednesday, and Friday evenings. Knowing that Doctor Almond preferred a first-come-first–serve system instead of appointments, patients would line up on the sidewalk in front of the office before the opening hour. After K or I unlocked the front door, we asked patients to sign the registry notebook sitting on the counter of the window opening that joined the waiting and nurse's rooms. We looked up patient files in the old metal file drawers or meticulously created 5"x7" cards for new patients, carefully writing down a name, address, and phone number, leaving space for Dad's notes and diagnosis below.

Usually Dad saw patients in the order they registered, but he always treated his allergy patients first so he could monitor them for an hour after they received their shots and he tried to not make pregnant women—his OB patients—wait since they came every month for checkups. And a very sick person or a screaming child would receive care quickly. Dad made sure he saw every person on the list, which meant he often worked long past closing time.

Patients sitting in the waiting room reflected the diverse population of our rural county—farmers, stay-at-home moms and their children, store-keepers, professors, students, coal miners, teachers, construction workers, the out-of-work, and the elderly. These patients brought the sterile office to life. Some were friendly and talkative. Others, quiet and reserved. Patients brought interesting smells with them, too. Sweat and dirt from the fields or the mines. Strong soap and shampoo. Occasionally a whiff of aftershave, perfume, booze, and tobacco. Sometimes, strong body odor permeated the rooms, coming from those who lived in homes with no running water.

Dad treated each patient equally with respect and courtesy. Though not a talkative man, he conveyed gentle concern. And there was his insatiable curiosity. He genuinely wanted to know what was wrong with his patients and he paid close attention. He asked lots of questions, always interested in making the right diagnosis, intrigued by unusual symptoms that might stump him, satisfied when he spotted something unusual. Most patient ailments were routine, but Dad saved lives in his office.

One evening, two men rushed into the office carrying a teenage boy who had stopped breathing. The older man quickly relayed that he was the manager of the theatre across the street.

"Doc. The kid swallowed a red fireball and it got stuck." Dad, at six feet and two hundred pounds, immediately picked up the teen by his feet and held him upside down. Asking the men to hold the boy, Dad thumped the boy on the back and the fireball flew out of the boy's mouth and across the room.

Another time, a stay-at-home mother and her three pre-school children came into the office and complained of severe daily headaches. After asking many questions about the family's activities and home life, Dad suspected that the family's house contained carbon monoxide. He called the Buckhannon Fire Chief and asked him if he could send an inspector out to the house. Sure enough, carbon monoxide was seeping into the house through an old heater.

Before patients left the office, they would pay Dad or us. He typically charged $5 or $10 for the office visit. Oftentimes, patients could not afford to pay even though they were grateful for the doctor's service. They would make an effort to repay the debt months later with a bushel of corn or a basket of tomatoes.

Occasionally, Dad would call us to come into the exam room to help with patient care. I liked weighing babies and giving the Boy Scouts their eye exams during their annual physicals. I didn't mind holding a small pan to catch water so Dad could wash out a patient's ear, but I felt queasy if Dad asked me to sit with a child getting a shot or to help bandage wounds. Once I almost passed out when I assisted with draining a large blister on a woman's leg.

Besides performing clerical duties and helping with medical exams, we went to the bank, gave kids lollipops, kept the waiting room straightened, and shared a cup of coffee with Dad. Above all, we talked with patients while they waited. They would tell us about their ailments, their families, their farms, and how they met Doctor Almond. With a steady stream of patients coming into the office, we were seldom bored.

Even though K and I never became nurses, working at Dad's office taught us the complexities of a small business and the importance of good communication skills. Most significantly, we learned how beloved and well-respected our Father was in our community and how hard he worked in his medical practice each day of his life.

CHRISTMAS HOUSE CALL
K

Dad loved to make house calls. So he said. And he said he loved to have us kids along, one at a time, if you please. I was a teenage girl, shy and quiet with my dad. And Dad was Dad. He was good at conversation if he picked the subject but otherwise he was mostly silent. I didn't have much give-and-take conversation in me. But Dad said, "Come along with me as I go to Pickens. Or Alton. Or Mud Lick. Or Swamp Run."

Christmas Day, 1963, I was 14 years old. "K, come along with me to Volga." We had already emptied our stockings. We'd had pancakes. The rest of our Christmas gifts would wait.

Off we went in Dad's trusty Jeep. Snow was falling. And at 7 a.m. it turns out no one had ventured forth. We were making the tracks all the way out Rt. 20 and onto Rt. 119 through Century. At the Volga Road we continued to be the only tracks.

I remember a coal company house up beside the road. An old woman hot and chilled and moaning. A shot of penicillin. "If you're not feeling better, come in to my office tomorrow morning." "Thank you, Doctor. I think I'm a mite better already."

Now the drive home. I felt so satisfied. Maybe we saved that old woman's life. Maybe we'd made her day.

I do not remember a single gift I received my 14th Christmas. Nor do I remember any gifts I gave. I'm not sure if Dad and I travelled in silence. I do know that Christmas drive in the snow and the simple care and compassion Dad showed make up my Christmas Memory for that year of my life.

OLD IRONSIDES
Greenbrier

"Spinner Hoover has a Live Oak growing on his property, thanks to Maurice Brooks planting it years ago. Greenbrier, if you get a leaf from that tree in your 4-H West Virginia Trees Project, you will get a blue ribbon for sure!" Dad exclaimed.

It was decided: our family would go on a call to French Creek. I loved when Dad got excited about a project. We usually gained more than we bargained for.

Mom had become the Upshurite 4-H Club Leader. We met in our living room monthly, crowding in over 30 kids. Earning a double major at West Virginia Wesleyan College in Biology and Home Economics made 4-H a perfect match for her. She agreed: scoring a *Quercus virginiana* P. Mill for the 4-H Tree Project would be super.

Driving up the road, we sang Johnny Horton's "Battle of New Orleans," a recent #1 hit on the Billboard Hot 100. Dad told us the history of the War of 1812, which included the Battle of New Orleans in 1815. He told us about the USS Constitution carved out of 25-inch-thick Live Oak planks. British cannonballs bounced off the ship's side, earning it the name "Old Ironsides." Mom told us about Maurice Brooks, a West Virginia University biology professor who planted an arboretum not only at French Creek but also at WVU in Morgantown.

Dad told us that Spinner Hoover made a great math teacher. His cousin, Beth Darnell, was the teacher under whom Mom did her student teaching in biology. In 1957 our sister Beth joined the Almond clan. Her name reflected the esteem Mom and Dad had for the Hoover/Darnell family. We loved both Beths.

Arriving soon enough at French Creek, where Grandfather Reverend Paul L. Flanagan preached on occasion in the historic Presbyterian church, we turned left across the creek and began our meandering climb, "following a cow path" as Dad noted. At the top of the ridge, giant oak, beech, maple, poplar, and other varieties of West Virginia trees grew in all their splendor. To me this place looked a lot like heaven as I imagined it to be.

We parked the Jeep on the ridge and trekked down into a cove. Below the bank, a giant Live Oak spread out in majesty and looked to be about 100 feet tall. My only other time to see Live Oaks had been during our vacation drive to Miami Beach, Florida, where Dad had attended the American Medical Association Annual Convention. In the south, the Live Oaks spread over the roads, and Spanish moss drapes the long horizontal branches. This we observed especially in St. Augustine, where we visited Ripley's Believe It or Not! Museum.

Here, farther north, the dark green, smooth leaves look polished, since they are not covered by Spanish Moss. How the Live Oak survived in our harsh Appalachian winters was a miracle, Dad figured. Mom credited Maurice Brooks with the good sense to plant deep in a cove, protecting the tree from the blasts of frigid wind.

Spinner Hoover stood, all smiles, pleased that Doc and his family had come on a tree call and not a house call. We collected leaves to press between pages of a Sears and Roebuck Catalog. We also gathered acorns.

"The acorn doesn't fall far from the tree," Spinner commented, repeating an old mountain proverb. He said that all five Almonds looked to be a cut off the old block. I told him that my parents had given me a piggy bank which had written on the side: "From little acorns, mighty oaks do grow." We told him that each of us had a savings account at the Adrian Buckhannon Bank for our college education.

Spinner Hoover said that deserved a southern treat of sweet tea, which he served to us on the wide veranda of his farmhouse. Then and there I determined to someday live in a home where giant shade trees welcome squirrels, song birds, and little children.

Wishing you a Holy Christmas and a Blessed New Year

Anne - Harold - Ruth -
'K' - Greenbrier -
+ Bethw was, too!

MOM

MOM WAS SAFE
Ruthie

My mom was the only daughter of her mother. Grandma was the second wife of a widowed preacher with six children. When Reverend Flanagan married Grandma, a career deaconess, she was almost 40 years old. The next year, 1922, Mom was born.

The situation shaped who Mom was. She was valued as a child, but expected to be good. Mom was self-disciplined. She was very smart—valedictorian of her high school class who went on to college, and graduated with a double major in biology and home economics. Mom was like a responsible, only child as well. This combination of self-discipline, intelligence, and responsibility would seem daunting, but also added to the combination was a deep kindness for and a strong love of people.

She had a solid, but continually growing faith in the Lord Jesus Christ and a strong belief in the Scriptures as truth.

Mom loved to learn. She read. She kept learning about nature and cultures around the world.

Mom was compassionate. She had a heart for those who were hurt—whether people, birds, or animals.

Mom practiced contentment. She was happy, daily, to be at home or in our little town.

She made good use of her time and worked hard, especially in managing our home. This enabled her to relax and listen whenever my dad or her five children needed to talk. She also had time to make friends and to be a friend.

Mom had a clear view of letting children be children. I think she liked the innocence that children had. She knew it was the adults' place to provide a safe place for children.

She respected boundaries. She never poked into my private letters or treasure boxes.

Besides always teaching us, her children, valuable work lessons, she read and re-read books and books to us. One of my favorite memories is seeing Mom read those same books to my boys, Joseph and Chris, when they were young.

This could be one of the reasons we five siblings wrote this book—so our children and grandchildren, and you, dear reader, could experience the joy of stories.

FIGURING OUT MOM
Anne

The way I would describe Mom depends on my age and hers.

As a 10-year-old, I would have described Mom as a nice and cheerful Mother who loved Daddy and us five kids more than anyone else in the world. She made family the center of her life. She ate lunch every day with Dad when he finished his office hours and greeted us when we came home from school. She loved her garden and the yard more than housecleaning. Our house itself was important—custom designed by Mom with built-ins and a fireplace in the big kitchen—but she cherished her flower garden. She liked having all our friends around, shooed us to play outside as much as possible, and invited lots of interesting guests to our house for Sunday dinner of chicken and mashed potatoes and fresh green peas.

When I grew older, Mom became the disciplinarian. She and I frequently disagreed. She strictly enforced church attendance, curfews, household responsibilities, and homework. She worried about her teenagers. She didn't allow me to go to the drive-in movies with boys, and she would sleep on the kitchen couch or wait up for me until I got home from a date. No alcohol. No smoking. No fooling around. On the other hand, she never objected to my short skirts or bleached hair or loud slumber parties, she never raised her voice in anger, and she proudly attended every play, every parade, every concert. And, those late night talks—over warm molasses cookies and milk—were frank and helpful.

In my twenties, I started a career and lived on my own. Mom cared for me from a distance, sending me her weekly, newsy, supportive, carbon-copied letters, with $5 tucked into the envelope, to New York or Ohio or Connecticut or Maryland. We even talked on the telephone occasionally. She became an advisor and nurturer during our long kitchen-sink talks when I returned home for visits. During that time, she often felt tired and worn out because she provided care for Grandma and Grandpa Flanagan who lived in our home the last five years of their lives. She appreciated having us visit so she could spend 30 minutes by herself—for a nap or a walk or to pull a few weeds.

At 33, I married Richard and we soon started our family. Mom and I truly connected as adults. Our value systems finally meshed and we began to agree on so many aspects of life. Mom became my go-to person with questions about child-raising. We enjoyed hiking downtown together, talking about all the homes we passed and stopping briefly so she could snap a picture of a Boggess Street flower or a Gum Street cat—pictures she would later attach to a card with a friendly note to the owner of said flower or cat. She and I often exchanged letters, recalling small incidents about our days and sharing private thoughts.

Mom shined as a grandmother. I remember her early morning talks with three-year-old Ginger. Just the two of them sitting at the kitchen table chatting away while everyone else slept. I can still see her reading bedtime stories to Jesse and Ginger and Chris (with Joseph and Taylor and Maria and Ronce listening in) as they all snuggled with Grandma on the couch. Her grandchildren adored her. She was their playmate ("Anyone ready for a game of dominoes?") and their teacher ("Who can find the Big Dipper tonight?") and their confidante ("Honey, I'm listening.") And I, as a young mother, could now fully appreciate the depth and capacity of my own Mother's love.

MOTHER MINE
K

Mother loved playing April Fool jokes. She would scheme and plan. Then giggle as she declared, "April Fool." One year (or maybe several) shortly after we three oldest all could dress ourselves, she sewed up our pants and the sleeves of our tops. It made for confusion and frustration. "April Fool." Just once she put salt in the sugar bowl. Dad howled! She hated making him upset but she never minded telling the tale. When Glenn and I were dating, she served him a big cup of coffee on this day. "With everything please." Milk and sugar. Her homemade pickle relish. Salt and catsup, mustard. "April Fool" with lots of giggles. Ah, Mother!

Another time, two college friends of mine were hiking the Appalachian Trail south of Harpers Ferry and called to ask me to rescue them for a few days of rest. Dave and Bob were glad for a place in our apartment behind the garage. They had several cans of beer in their backpacks which they tucked into the fridge in the apartment. They didn't know that Mom hated alcohol of any kind and that the fridge was an extra one for our big family. When she stopped by to get another gallon of milk, she saw the Budweiser and immediately threw the cans in the trash. She put a quart jar of her delicious homemade tomato juice in the fridge with a photo-note with the words, "Cheers. Lois Almond."

We often walked to Sunday School. Down the length of Victoria Street then down Florida. Somehow we always had a few extra minutes to scurry under the mulberry tree on the corner of Victoria and Florida. It was a neat hiding place; Mom would crawl in with us. A neighbor lady told her kids, who later told me, "That Lois Almond! All she does is play with her kids!"

Frank Berisford told me years after Mom's death, "Your mom could only say good things about others. If we were talking about the Devil, Lois would say, 'He sure is a hard worker.'"

Mother loved having fun. And she loved sharing fun. We would gather Queen Anne's Lace and turn them blue and green and pink and yellow. Ditto to eggs at Easter. We each had our own flower bed and could plant there whatever we wanted. Every night she read poems and stories from *Childcraft*,

Freckles, *My Friend Flicka*, or *Swiss Family Robinson*.

Mom loved to read the Sunday comics; she loved to recite poems and sing songs. "I never saw a Purple Cow. I never hope to see one; but I can tell you anyhow, I'd rather see than be one," and "Spring has sprung. The grass is riz. I wonder where the birdies is. The bird is on the wing. Why, that's absurd. Last time I heard, the wings were on the bird." She would belt out this song about her beloved Chicago: "One dark night when we were all in bed, Old Mother Leary left the lantern in the shed. When the cow kicked it over, she winked one eye and said, 'We'll have a hot time in the Old Town tonight.'"

I remember Mom with her older sisters, Julia and Martha, or with her friends Ella Bea and Irma, or with the Lunch Bunch, giggling and giggling and giggling.

Mother loved having fun. *Joy* was her touch word. She especially loved going on walks with her Honey, our Dad. The path around our property was well worn.

But Mother was also disciplined and opinionated, teaching her children life values and responsibility. We kids all had our Chore List and then an extra list if we wanted to earn money. We had piano lessons with at least ½ hour of practice each day. We could go outside after homework was done. Mom would spend hours with each of us doing spelling words and the multiplication tables. Sunday School and Worship were givens. 4-H was a must. As well as Loyal Temperance Legion and Youth Temperance Council.

Each day after school we would gather around our round kitchen table and with the milk and homemade cookies would come the question, "What did you learn today?" "Do you agree with that?" Mom could get a good argument going in no time! And she had her opinions. She was out to save her corner of the world. She loved wholesome living. No alcohol. No strip mining. No tobacco or other drugs. No abortions. She had no time for card playing and would toss away any cards she found, but she loved Rook and Old Maid. She would not let us go to the movies or swimming on Sundays, for that caused someone to work on the Sabbath.

But somehow Mother had an accepting heart. She seemed to love each person she met and was truly interested in their lives.

Spare children. Troubled teens. Homesick international students. Folks all over Buckhannon who needed a start of one of her iris or shasta daisies or who needed a note of encouragement or gratitude with a photo of their front door. Mom was accepting of people. Just as she found them, or as they could become.

KIND TO A FAULT
Greenbrier

Mom was kind to a fault.

Mom wanted me to befriend the friendless on the playground. That would risk my standing as a "cool Joe," the way I saw it. My classmate Bob suffered from polio and thus moved awkwardly and mumbled. Heeding Mom's advice, I did stand by him during an ice skating playground disaster (as recounted in the story "The Barrister's Bookcase and the Traveler's Wooden Trunk" in my book *Stories of a West Virginia Doctor's Son*). We became friends, and that guided my practice of medicine in caring for the developmentally challenged and neurologically impaired. Now I embrace her philosophy, rooting for the underdog in sports and in life.

Mom wanted me to go out of my way to meet the new students. That would have been okay most of the time, but sometimes I met kids on the edge. In high school Dave moved to town. He had moved almost every year of his life. Walking down to the Dairy Queen one summer day, Dave asked me if I could hear the bells chiming out a musical song. No, I could not. As I sat next to him in church one Sunday, he began to call out with a plaintive cry that he wanted to be like Jesus. I did too, but I did not know what to do with his emotional anguish. Shortly after these events, Dave was admitted to West Virginia University Hospital, suffering a "nervous breakdown." Years later as a psychiatrist, I met many "Daves" in the ER, sticking with them as they battled demons and chronic mental illness.

Mom wanted me to date girls who, for want of a better word, were "wallflowers." In my senior year at B-UHS, I was president of the Quill and Scroll International Honorary Society for high school journalism students. I was searching for a money-making project. By chance one day, Nora Amundson, our French teacher, burst out in frustration when we had one more assembly devoted to one more event that would take us out of class:

"The next thing you know, we will be electing a Jelly Bean Queen!"

Right then and there I determined, indeed, we *would* elect a Jelly Bean Queen. It would be a great project for the Quill and

Scroll. Gaston's Wholesale Grocery could supply us with 1,000 pounds of jelly beans. We members would then package them in little sandwich bags that we would sell to members of the student body for 10 cents each. The bags each had a ballot inside that could be used for a write-in vote for the Jelly Bean Queen. A joke is a joke, but the joke took a nasty turn when ballot stuffing began for "wallflower" girls. In the end, one of the most popular girls, appropriately named Claudia Bean, became our first and only Jelly Bean Queen.

Mom wanted us to be kind to deprived inner-city children. Each year our family sold Christmas trees we had grown on our property for $1.00 a tree. Our family project with the profits when I was in the sixth grade was to bring age-matched kids from Pittsburgh to Buckhannon for a green vacation. These children were part of the foster care and orphanage system, and experienced firsts such as horseback riding and swimming in a river. The boy matched with me was a budding juvenile delinquent and told some pretty raunchy jokes. Mom was kind, but once again there were some unintended consequences. Now I practice medicine, helping children who have been abused and neglected. Also, I am currently a member of the Upshur County Board of Education, my goal being to provide a quality public education for all children.

Mom was kind to a fault. I thank her from the bottom of my heart for the way she raised K, Anne, Ruth, Beth, and me!

MY MOTHER-OF-PEARL
Beth

Let's just get these things out of the way, right from the start, dear. My mother hated two things: alcohol and strip mining. By religious convictions, she didn't like taking the Lord's name in vain, going to the movies or the like on Sunday, gambling, any harm to God's Holy Temple (our bodies), or laziness in herself or others.

But Mother had a subtleness about her that was endearing. For example, when I would be asked to sell raffle tickets for school, she would write a note to the teacher: "I am returning Bethie's tickets. We do not believe in gambling. Oh, but here is a donation for your fund-raiser." Point taken, gift given, child spared most of the embarrassment. If she found a deck of cards on one of the cluttered shelves in my room, she would simply dump them in the trash can—no punishment, but once again, point taken. Her letters to the local newspaper editors about environmental abuse of the West Virginia wildness she loved would focus on a viable alternative, a sadness with a plea rather than an attack. And even though she would rubber-stamp her envelopes "Outlaw Alcohol," she graciously accepted the local mead maker's gift of wine (after making it clear she didn't drink) and then put it unopened in the garbage. Her motto back in college was "Lips that touch wine will never mine!"

My mother was the embodiment of the (4)"Hs" of 4-H and especially of their slogan, "to make the best better." The Head "H" was the emphasis on education and commonsense. This included her knowledge of wildflowers and her crackerjack ability to come up with wacky puns. The Heart "H" was her amazing acceptance and love of all God's children and creatures and especially her love of Dad, her family, her home, and her parents. The Hand "H" worked the vegetables and flower gardens, arranging bouquets for shut-ins and the church altar. The hands fixed meals for the family and always the extra guests at the table. They sewed matching Valentine's Day pajamas for her five children, year after "mumu" year. Health "H" was exemplified by walking, fresh air, abstinence, temperance, ping pong games, good choices and habits.

Above all else, Mother maintained a high level of Joy, her favorite word and her favorite emotion. I was blessed with a mother who looked for the good in a person as an individual, a unique child of God. There may have been a touch of the "hate the sin," but her personal credo overwhelmingly yielded to love the sinner.

My mother could answer the doorbell to find two clean-cut, tie-straight Mormon missionaries on our doorstep and, within minutes, they understood she was a die-hard Methodist, she accepted who they were, and would they like to come for supper one night this week since they were obviously new to town. And would they mind telling the family what it was like to grow up in Utah, Idaho, or wherever? The epitome of West Virginia hospitality, she was the queen of "there's always room at our table."

It was this trait of my mother's that I yearned to emulate—find the common ground, recognize the inner spark, be willing to overlook the quirks and differences, but never lose sight of one's self. As she would say, "We have much to learn from others and they, in turn, from us."

 "Glory to God in the highest, and on earth peace, good will toward men."

St. Luke 2:14

FIRST DAY OF SUMMER

THE WHOLE SUMMER AHEAD
Anne

What a glorious thought! "I don't have to get up now." As the sound of noisy birds and the smell of fresh grass float through my open window, I roll over in bed.

Naturally, I can't get back to sleep and ten minutes later I hop out of bed, planting my bare feet on the cool oak floor. I slip on flowered shorts and a top that Mom created from old curtains. (Years later, I wondered when she found time to make our dresses, shirts, coats, pajamas, and pants. She spent many late nights at her sewing machine.)

After quickly brushing my teeth, observing the only hard and fast rule of summer mornings, I run down our long hallway. Where is everyone? The kitchen is empty and quiet. Once again, I am the last one up. Only my bowl, a box of cereal, and a lone glass of orange juice greet me. Gulping the juice, I race outside. The wet dewy grass tickles my toes.

Hearing noises in the garage, I see Greenbrier and K getting down the halter and saddle. Full of anticipation that only the beginning of summer can bring, we lug the heavy equipment to the pasture to find our gentle old horse Pinto Scout who was always ready to give us a slow ride around the property. Brier barks happily as he runs beside us. We lead Pinto to the bench that Uncle Paul and Dad built for us and hoist ourselves high up on the soft leather saddle—often two or three of us at a time—and head straight toward a whole summer of lazy days.

Pinto, sensing our excitement, gives us a surprisingly frisky ride. After we feed him breakfast, we find Mom to tell her we are heading up the hill to play. Our neighborhood has seven houses and fifteen kids. It's spread out over a quarter mile and our gravel road is a dead end. Nice and quiet except for our shrieks and hollers.

The dads keep the big lawns mowed, which makes certain activities just right for each house. We play baseball in the Daniels' backyard and croquet in our front yard. We climb Mrs. Stansberry's trees, and, in the winter, sled down the Brooks' hill. A perfect playground. Usually, Mom doesn't have a problem with us roaming the neighborhood as long as we tell her where we are going.

Today, though, she says we can leave "as soon as you do your chores. The list is beside the telephone." Groaning, we run back in the house to scan the dreaded list. I'm in luck. All I have for today is to mop the downstairs and help Bethie with her bath tonight. For now, I get the mop from the corner of the utility room and swish through each room, making sure I mop under all the beds and under the couches. Mom will probably check there later and I do not want to mop again!

Soon, K and I head up to the Daniels' house to look for Greenbrier who managed to cut through his chores quickly. We take our usual path up the hill through the Brooks' backyard to yell "Hey" to Timmy and pick up Jeff. Then past the Lockwoods' trailer and the Clarks' big white house. We wave to Mrs. Stansberry, our favorite neighbor, as she weeds her vegetable garden under the late morning sun. We eye her big hemlock tree and make plans to climb it on our return home.

As we near the Daniels' house, we see the gang already playing softball. We are so excited knowing this will be the first of dozens of activities together over the summer. Today, the whole gang is here—Patsy, Jeannie, Danny, Percy, George, Gene, Greenbrier, Jeff, K, and me. I'm the youngest in the Mt. Hibbs Gang so I have to run fast to keep up. Later in the summer, the younger kids—Ruthie, David, John Brent, Timmy, and Bethie—will join us for birthday parties and watermelon feasts.

After a noisy game, we bid the Daniels good-bye, promising to return on Saturday. The Daniels own the only television set in the neighborhood, so they let us all come and sit on their living room floor on Saturday mornings to watch *Roy Rogers*, *Rin Tin Tin*, and the best show of all, *The Lone Ranger*.

For now, we run home for a lunch of chicken soup and oyster crackers. Sitting around the table, we happily plan our afternoon adventure. Should we play in the City Park where it's cooler? Walk the Enchanted Forest path? Climb the Clarks' apple trees? Hike to the top of Mt. Hibbs? Explore the haunted house? Suddenly, we break into a fit of giggles. We have plenty of time to get all of these important things done. We have the whole summer ahead.

COME OUT AND FEEL THE WORLD
K

"School's out! School's out! Teacher let the fools out." What will I do with My Whole Entire Life that unfolds before me? Today I will take it easy. Third grade at Academy with Mrs. Brake. Finished. Sleeping in until 8:30 a.m. Done.

Mom is pregnant, due in mid-July. It is also the summer when Uncle Walter and his son Sonny and his friend Freddy Braun are building Dad's office. Mom feeds them every evening and prepares their beds and washes their dirty clothes. Freddy is a 17-year-old cutie, and Anne and I giggle and flirt and dream of him. He is amused and very patient.

Our kitchen is Grand-Central in the early morning and every evening. Now it is quiet so I sit on the sofa by the windows and ponder my summer as I drink my OJ. I think of our trip to New Jersey and New York for an AMA Medical Association meeting, Vacation Bible School, Loyal Temperance Legion camp, and lots of overnights with my friends Barbie Bea, and Janet, and Cathy.

But the Here and Now is here and now; I will do my chores for the day. Sweeping the kitchen and the basement steps. Picking a row of beans. Looking at the tomatoes, not quite ripe. Making a bouquet of sweet peas, wild and tame for the center of the kitchen table. Practicing the piano for ½ hour. No, all that can wait. It is the start of Summer Vacation.

I run outside and "feel the world." I shout next door to my friend Jeff. "What's up? Come on over." Greenbrier is already washing Brier. Anne loves to sleep, so she is still in her room. Ruth cannot even blissfully imagine the import of this day since she won't start in kindergarten for two whole years.

Why waste another minute? I run barefooted in the green, green grass of that free May day. Jeff is here and we decide to start in the sandbox. (Thank you, Dad, for taking us up to Ten Mile last weekend to get some fresh white sand which greets us in the sandbox.) Jeff and I create mountains and valleys and tunnels and buildings. Some twigs of spruce and pine and peach and apple for the woods. The roads are curvy West Virginia specials. The imaginary town we build is typical: a one-room school, a church, a post office-grocery-gas station all in one, and little houses with some outbuildings all around. Brier ambles by and shakes after his bath. Greenbrier aims the hose right at K- and Jeff-Ville. Streams and rivers cut through our masterpiece. Hey! Looks like the right place for a Mud Pie Factory. Watch out, Greenie.

SIMPLE PLEASURES
Greenbrier

"School's out, school's out! Teacher let the mules out!"

We chant and then scream in glee as we push open the large double doors of Academy Grade School and run for the playground. Sandy Mick swings the highest. Brent Reed swings his younger sister higher and higher. I stand up and swing with feet planted on the seat, playing trapeze artist. Mike Adams dares me to jump, but having just healed from a broken arm, I'm a little cautious, though I know that I can do a flying leap almost to the giant maple tree shading us.

Such freedom!

Such joy!

As school buses arrive to take home my schoolmates who live out in the country, I feel a tinge of sadness that school is out. The separation anxiety is real. Our goodbyes are a bit melodramatic. We promise to be friends forever and to see each other in the fall.

Miss Swisher, my third grade teacher, let us watch the Disney film *The Adventures of Huck Finn* at school's end. I found the dialogue between Jim and Huckleberry Finn amusing. How I love discovering Mark Twain! Maybe on a rainy day in the coming summer bliss I can read about Tom Sawyer's adventures.

Now, off I run to meet my sisters at the school crossing. K and Annie are waiting on the corner of College Avenue and Kanawha Street. We will use our nickels Mom has given us to buy Popsicles at Reger's Store. We laugh and jostle for position in front of the old couple, as we wave our treats and our change in the air, begging for service.

Orange is my favorite flavor. Sucking our frozen rewards, we head down Kanawha Street and turn up Victoria Hill. It's time to stop and visit Grandmother and Grandfather Flanagan. My orange Popsicle melts, but I hold on to the stick. Mom will put our sticks in an ice cube tray and pour in orange Kool-Aid for homemade frozen treats. Over on the counter next to the coal fireplace, Grandmother has homemade orange peel candy, just in time for a refresher supply of orange.

First, Grandmother wants to see our report cards. She asks whether or not we passed. I do not even know, so I am sure glad when she says that I did.

My, my, fourth grade in the fall.

Ugh!!!

Let's not think of school. Summer is here. May it last forever.

SUMMER OF '71
Beth

"Oh, man, Dinah, why are you sitting on the edge of my bed, staring at me? Let me sleep. What time is it anyway?"

My best friend and pseudo-sister was a "hop-out-of-bed and do fifty laps around the gym" kind of gal. I, on the other hand, walked into walls and could take a nap in the shower. But she had a point, wanting me to rise and shine in the early morning on this our first day of summer vacation. When we headed back to school after Labor Day, our lives would be different. Junior High. Ninth grade. The highest folks on the totem pole at last. First team sports. Student Council leadership roles. First chairs in band. Responsibility. But this was our summer and the beginning was Now.

I gritted my teeth as I looked over the daily chore list sitting by my cereal bowl and glass of orange juice. With the older siblings gone and Grandma living with us, that numbered piece of paper often represented a feeling of jail time before parole: sweep the glassed-in porch with its many leaf-shedding plants; dust all the window sills in a house with dozens of windows; vacuum the living room, a space where fifty 4-H'ers met the Monday before; run the dust mop over the hardwood floors of five bedrooms, a den, and a long hallway. The last item was practice the piano for thirty minutes, and perhaps I could negotiate that one for later in the day when friends would gather around the piano as I attempted to play the pop culture songs and they would bellow out the words to Joni Mitchell's "Both Sides Now."

I sighed and Dinah picked up a magazine. Her mother never gave her chores and I knew she would only help towards the end of the hour or so, as we both grew anxious to head out and meet up with our friends.

This first day was not about following our likely routine for the upcoming summer, rather this was a day to simply get our groove, feel things out, put our toes into the waters of what was cool in this summer of 1971. Things were changing quickly in our small insulated world of hilly Appalachia. Our music tastes were differing from the bubble gum of The Archies to the mesmerizing rhythmics of Jimi Hendrix. We took masking tape and cut out stencils of boys' names, put them on our tummies and rubbed baby oil on them—summer tattoos of an enduring, but not permanent nature. The same could be said for the peroxide and Sun-In sprayed into hair that first day of summer. Many friends sported gorgeous highlights while I ached with tangerine Bozo hair.

We scouted out our sleep-out spot for the night, hooking up with Amy next door, and wandering down into the pine forest below the house. The heat of a West Virginia summer was a time of freedom, for sleeping one night inside and then one night outside. We learned to wander in the night at an early age, never seeming to fear what or whom we might stumble upon, unless there was an escapee from Weston State Hospital, fifteen miles away.

It was about this age, this time period, that secrets were buried in many ways, including the literal packs of cigarettes, wrapped in brown paper sacks, tucked under rocks deep in the Enchanted Forest. Ours was not an adolescence of innocence, not by this time, not with rules so easily broken. We watched television, we traveled to big cities and heard tales of others that were now burning; we learned of fashion and hippies and war. We read books and saw movies that stretched our worlds. Sex, drugs, and rock 'n' roll found their way to our mountains and, as we stepped out to begin our summer vacation, we started a journey into a place previously unknown. We were lucky. We were safe. We were loved and watched over by our small town mothers and fathers and our community. Our roots were steeped in discipline and hard work, but our branches were not pruned.

SUMMER PLANS
Ruthie

Oh, to finally be able to sleep in with no alarm clock waking me! This is the first day of summer vacation. My white cat, Popcorn, snuggles beside me as I lie a minute longer in bed. My little sister, Beth, is just starting to stir. Mom is brewing coffee for Dad. The smell drifts upstairs through the open window. The birds chirp in the crisp dew-soaked air here at our hilltop home in the mountains of West Virginia. The sun brightly shines, inviting me to get up.

What joy to think about the plans for the summer that stretches ahead. Fourth grade is finished. This summer's plans include my first 4-H camp. Greenbrier, K, and Anne have been going for years. Finally I will be allowed to stay all week long, not just travel with Daddy up to drop the older ones off, and return with him Friday night for the campfire and dark trip home.

This year I will have stories to tell Mom and Dad about camp adventures and new skills. I think archery and swimming in the Buckhannon River top my list.

However, camp is more than a month away. I need to finish my 4-H project. My perfect batch of cookies might win a blue ribbon this coming weekend at the judging of all the dozens of 4-H projects other Upshur County youth plan to display. The display is part of the yearly Strawberry Festival with parades, exhibits, and the carnival.

That thought motivates me to move toward getting up to seek Mom out for a list of chores to earn some spending money. Will the list include washing windows, pulling weeds, dusting, or cleaning out the garage?

Next to my bed is the new Nancy Drew mystery I want to start today. Perhaps later in the afternoon the younger neighborhood kids will show up for a pick-up game of softball. We can play until the moms begin to call them home for supper: "John Brent," "David," "Donna," "Amy Jane." If the new family across the fields comes, we will have four more counting little Tappy, their only girl.

After supper, perhaps Beth and I can catch some sparkling fireflies before our tub bath. It is nice that she is finally old enough to go on family vacation later this summer. All of us in Atlantic City on the beach—hopefully it will be great fun.

Thus begins my first day of summer after the end of the school year. Ahead is camp, Strawberry Festival, reading of books, swimming and bike riding, the company of cousins, chores, and cookies to bake.

I put on my new, blue cat-eye glasses that bring the world into focus, and go downstairs to greet Daddy. He says, "Hey, feller. Top of the morning!" And it was top of the summer. Glorious freedom.

Season's Greetings

The Almond Family

A WALK REMEMBERED

HOME AGAIN. HOME AGAIN.
K

I remember camping at the Wilderness alone when I was about 19. Where did I ever get that notion? To stay all night alone in that tucked-away little cabin and to walk the 19 miles home the next morning? Greenbrier drives me up to the Wilderness on a Friday evening. Yes, I have matches, a potato, a steak, coffee and eggs for the morning. Kindling is everywhere; the mattress looks mouse-free for now and fresh water is in the well. "So long. See you later."

A peaceful evening unfolds. No sign of any people. Almost no sign of any beasts or hungry critters. The stream is high and the noise of rushing water drowns out the sounds of all but the closest birds. "What cheer! What cheer! Birdie. Birdie. Birdie. Birdie."

After a night of quiet sleep and a morning of fire-building, coffee drinking, and straightening up the simple, simple cabin, with the sign on the door "Enter as a stranger only once," I take off from Hemlock to Buckhannon. I know I'll walk through Upper Queens with all the Zickefooses, then Lower Queens with the wide fishing hole and lovely bridge, then to Tallmansville, then on past the Tenney strawberry farm in the big bend, then on past Red Knob and Hickory Flat, past the high school, through Tennerton, and on home to West Victoria Drive.

But I best think only of a mile or so at a time. I love the road beside the Middlefork out of the Wilderness but it is all up. Then the "main road" through Hemlock is up, up, up. Finally I'm on Hemlock Ridge Road.

I walk briskly. I look all around into the woods and up top the hillside where Mother Skunk is preening her two little ones. I listen and can hear all the birds. I wave at the few folk getting ready to mow their yards or plant their spring gardens. I am glad to have a canteen of water. That cool fresh water from the Wilderness sure goes down smoothly.

Am I afraid? Am I lonely? Do I doubt that I can do it? No, no, and no. It is a time in my favorite place, doing one of my favorite things, with one of my very favorite people.

Then comes the rain, actually an April thunder and lightning storm. I don't mind getting wet but by the time I am soaked through to my underwear, I get nervous about the lightning.

I am approaching Tallmansville. I don't know who stopped. An old guy and his old wife. "Lassie, care for a ride?" "Don't mind if I do"—and I get in the backseat, with apologies for all the dampness. I have a dry and happy ride that last nine miles into Buckhannon. "I know where Doc Almond lives. I'll take you home."

Thank you, neighbors, whoever you are, for the welcomed ride—part of my walk remembered.

GOOD FOR WHAT AILS YOU
Greenbrier

Hiking to the Wilderness waterfall remains special every time I follow the path along the river, but never as fondly remembered as the first time. Finally, Mom and Dad had purchased the Warren T. and Matilda Braine Farm, with money inherited from Grandfather Henry David Almond's estate, in 1964. However, in my heart I loved the Wilderness at first sight from the time Brier, our Collie, and I made a country call with Dad in the summer of 1958 between fourth and fifth grade.

Taking title to the land, while fitting since our family so loved the place, did not make my heart skip a beat like my first walk to the waterfall. Cecil Hoover, a faithful neighbor to the Braine couple, suggested that Dad, Brier, and I walk down the trail to the falls because it would cure what ailed us. My heart was heavy that day because my good friend Ricky had just died in a farm accident. The Hoovers knew about grief, for they had lost their neighbor Warren and now daily checked on Matilda, as her heart failed. She had been born in the log cabin, then married Warren, and they had lived a peaceful and loving life for 50 years in the same homestead. What ailed the Hoovers as they trekked over the mountain, two miles as the crow flies, was that sense of a foreshortened future. Stopping at the waterfall proved refreshing. There is something eternal in hearing rushing water mold solid rock a grain of sand at a time.

Dad took me on this call to Hemlock to talk to me man to man. He lost his brother to a skin infection when Dad was my age, he shared. He knew my pain and grief. The Braine Farm was the most beautiful farm in Upshur County, Dad observed, as we turned off the rock-based road and headed down a mossy, damp lane into a deep and dark forest of mature hardwoods. A country mile down the trail, a gate stopped us. While opening and closing the gate, we picked red raspberries planted along the fence. Dad ate a few, then asked me to cup my hands, and he filled my paws. They tasted good mixed with the salt of my tears. I told Dad of Ricky's invitation to join Cub Scouts. He also planned to join the Upshurite 4-H Club when old enough. We had plans to camp together on his farm that summer. Dad listened to our boyhood plans never to be realized. We approached the ancient farmhouse made partly of log and partly of clapboard. Dad attended to Mrs. Braine, who looked so frail. Afterward he said we should walk to the waterfall and talk more.

Mr. Hoover pointed to the path down through the garden to a stile—wooden steps on which to climb over the fence—and into the back pasture. Dad remarked that he was feeling old and creaky as he slowly climbed over. Across the meadow we headed toward the rhododendron thicket along the Middle Fork River. In the shade at the far end, the moss grew so abundantly that Dad said it would be a perfect mattress for an overnight campout if I'd get a few friends together. Nodding my head yes, I plumped down in the finest carpet in West Virginia.

I reminded Dad of our trip to Charleston. He had attended a medical meeting at the Daniel Boone Hotel, and Mom walked all of us kids to the State Capitol to visit Governor Underwood. When Mom inquired with the Governor's secretary about us saying "How do you do?" and paying our respects, she was disappointed that he was out of the office. Boldly, Mom pointed out that we had walked a long way. Could we at least go into his office and sit in his chair? Yes, came the reply from the friendly secretary. So all of us took turns sitting in the big leather high-back chair. I even spun it around a few times.

"I do declare, Dad, while the Governor's office had thick carpet, the moss at the Braine Farm has it beat hands down."

Brier even took some tumbles with me as we rolled over and over on the carpet of moss. Then we headed down a narrow-gauge railroad bed. Dad commented that the track ran down five miles to Queens. Upstream it ran to High Germany and Upshur Mountain before crossing over the mountain, eventually heading for Elkins. Chestnut and other hardwoods had been worth the effort to harvest this wilderness forest.

"Gee, Dad, this is like corduroy pants, with the logs laid side by side." Indeed, he pointed out that the trees had been so abundant that logs served as the rail bed. I hopped and skipped down the trail to a bridge abutment with a washed-out bridge.

"Look at the ford in the stream," Dad instructed. "The train would need a trestle to cross. The engineers always build triangles for support, since that is the strongest geometric figure there is." Dad got excited, as he'd only seen corduroy roads like this in New Hampshire, when he spent seven years helping construct the Appalachian Trail as part of the Civilian Conservation Corps (CCC) during the Great Depression.

Since the track crossed the stream, but without a bridge, we stayed on the riverbank, entering a wall of rhododendron. We climbed up and down and around every which way, following our ears toward the sound of rushing water. At the end of the thicket we spied our prize that Mr. Hoover spoke of: a 10-foot waterfall cascading grandly after a recent summer rainstorm. The water hit sandstone boulders at the top and the bottom and sprayed off them, forming a series of arching rainbows. I could see where the pot of gold would be in a far-off clump of rhododendron.

Dad and I sat down on a rock ledge, looking down on the waterfall. We came under the magic spell of nature. The wonder of it all! He put his hand in mine and held it like he did Mother's. We sat in silence. There was no more talk about Ricky, but I knew everything was going to be all right.

What a walk to remember!

WALK ON, MY CHILDREN
Beth

Somehow, we never expected our mother to die. Not at the young age of 74. Not the woman who walked several miles most days nearly every day of her life. Not someone who had encouraged our own walking by refusing to drive a car after her oldest child got his driver's license. Mother would point to far-off buildings when we vacationed in cities such as Chicago or New York City and say, "Let's walk to there and back today." Her idea for fun on trips to Atlantic City would include supper at the restaurant at the end of the boardwalk, an hour away—an opportunity to work up an appetite. The walk back, of course, would be an aid to digestion. Our father and mother dated by taking walks up and down the hills surrounding their college town, nestled in the Buckhannon River valley of West Virginia.

The day before Mom's funeral, there was no need for discussion of what we, her children, needed to do to quiet the roar in our minds and heal the hole in our hearts. Along with our father, we took the back road journey twenty miles up to the Wilderness, in Hemlock. Our family retreat for over 50 years, the Wilderness is comprised of 125 acres—a typical mountain farm of about 20 flat acres, steep ridges up both sides, and a river, with a waterfalls, running through it.

After settling our elderly father in a comfortable lawn chair, a son-in-law sitting nearby, we five children set out to walk our property lines. It was a June day, a Sunday when the only church we dared to visit was this cathedral of Nature; our altars were the stones piled high by some long-ago pioneer clearing a hillside meadow for an apple orchard. Our hymns that day started with an old folk song often sung at family gatherings: "Oh, the Lord's been good to me. And so I thank the Lord, for giving me the things I need, the sun, the rain, and the apple seed. Oh, the Lord's been good to me. Amen." Instead of the usual rousting music, our voices and enthusiasms were half-hearted.

On we trudged, following the faint traces of old logging roads as we wound our way up the steep sides, reaching back to grab a hand and haul the one behind us over a fallen tree or a rocky crevice. Arriving at the top of the eastern ridge, we hiked the dirt road we were never allowed to call by its local name, "N-- Ridge Road," supposedly a path on the Underground Railroad. A few tentative smiles emerged as someone remarked, "Wasn't it just like Mom to rename this road 'Emancipation Boulevard'?"

Munching on nuts and apples, none of us planning for the very real need of food for endurance on a 125-acre hike, we doggedly began our first descent down the hillside to the mountain stream, the Left Fork of the Right Fork of the Middle Fork River (or whatever fork it might be). We crossed over near one of the bubbling springs, a spot where the Celtic ancestry in my genes often imagined the domiciles of wee people or fairies, if, indeed, such exist. Our mother was a Flanagan, typical of the Irish with her clear green twinkling eyes and rosy cheeks.

The western ridge looked high, but not as daunting. Our industry over the years in the planting of a wild flower garden on the lane (a noble attempt to have a patch of native botanicals), had obviously been discovered and considered by the plentiful deer as a tasty café. The mountain delicacies, ramps, were dug over here—patches of dark green leaves dotting the hillside. It was this side of the holler, down another logging road, where I imagined a tree house, complete with a front porch and a rocking chair. I dreamed of a place to meditate and view the waterfalls—and soak in the roar of the stream as it careened over the big rocks and ledges, making its strangely northward and westward journey toward the Ohio and then Mississippi Rivers.

The birds were eerily quiet on that solemn, soothing walk through the woods. The words of the poet Robert Frost echoed through my every foot fall. We had miles left to travel and promises still to uphold. Mother's encouraging voice came through those verses, too. "Yes, dears, you do have many more miles to travel and an abundance of promises to uphold. Walk on, my children. Walk on."

FRIENDSHIP LANE
Ruthie

Recently I took a walk down a long country road that leads to a farm. The road was a dirt, single lane with fences on each side. The road went through a wooded area and a pasture where dairy cows had once contentedly lived. I was remembering back to almost 50 years ago when, as a young teen, I first took that walk.

I was privileged to be part of the Upshur County band program from fifth grade through high school. I never played the clarinet very well, as our patient band directors Mr. Lawson and Mr. Puffenbarger would have told you. My joy from being in the band was in developing some dear friendships, of which I still reap the benefits to this day.

One such friendship began in seventh grade. Over the summer, Beth Ann had moved to Upshur County to live with her grandparents. She played the flute. Her grandparents' home was zoned for children to continue in seventh and eighth grades at the local elementary school. Other children in other parts of the county were bussed to either the one junior high school or the one high school, starting in seventh grade. However, since the only band program was in the junior high school, Beth Ann was allowed to come on the bus into Buckhannon.

Central West Virginia did not have much of a diversity of families in the 1960s. Most people were white of Anglo-Saxon background. Nevertheless, there was still a divide. There were the "town kids" and the "country kids." This division was not based on economics or education since there were poor in both places, and people of means both in town and throughout the county.

My father, who was raised near New York City with a huge variety of people groups, refused to divide people into ethnic or racial or other categories. As a doctor, he had patients from all over both town and country.

He and Mom encouraged us, their five children, to also have friendships based on more than where families lived. We were active in 4-H, so we got to know other kids from all over the county. However, I had gone from kindergarten through sixth grade with one group of town kids. So, seventh grade provided an opportunity to make some new friends.

One of these was Beth Ann. My dad and her grandparents knew each other, so Beth Ann was allowed to come home with me on Fridays to stay overnight. This was one of the most common adolescent girls' social activities during my youth. We could walk to the movies, or go to a high school football game, or just hang out and talk and talk. Dad would then drive Beth Ann home on Saturday afternoon after his office hours.

One weekend, Beth Ann invited me to come to her home. I had rarely ridden a school bus, so that ride began quite an adventure for me.

Her grandparents lived in a farmhouse that was not near other homes. Greta and Pap greeted us warmly. We had a delicious homemade supper with a special dessert. Then, as it grew dark, we played checkers before bedtime. Beth Ann's bedroom was up a steep flight of stairs. It was very quiet out in the country.

The next morning, after a breakfast with farm-fresh eggs, Beth Ann and I put on our boots to go for a visit to her best friend, Martha. She and Beth Ann had gotten to know each other over the many summers that Beth Ann and her mom had visited Greta and Pap before Beth Ann's mom died.

We walked a long way on a one-lane black-topped road, past another farmhouse and several fields. Then we began the real walk.

We opened a gate to a lane that stretched before us. There were puddles, ruts and grass growing in the middle of a vehicle path. I had been with Daddy on medical calls to farmhouses, so this was not totally unfamiliar. We went up a bit of a hill and through an area shaded by woods, then around a bend and out onto a view of a wide-open valley. There were milk cows fenced in on both sides of us and a big barn stood up ahead. To one side of the barn was a nice-looking farmhouse with a vegetable garden beside it.

Martha came out to greet us. I remember she showed us the barn and the milking machines. Then her kind mother welcomed us.

After a few hours, Martha walked Beth Ann and me back to the main road. I realized then that she walked that long lane every morning, rain or shine, even in the snow and dark, to catch the school bus. She also walked that same lane home after school.

There were milking and farm chores for her to do before school and again after school. That lane would change from season to season—fall leaves, deep snow, spring rains, wild flowers. And always those gentle cows. Those cows, familiar ladies, were a lot of work. Cleaning them before milking. Stalls to muck out. Big milk cans to lift. Heavy bales of hay, which the family had harvested and laid up in that barn, to feed the cows with in winter. Farming was a lot of work for the whole family, including young Martha.

That walk I took as an adolescent was the beginning of opening my eyes to ways of living that were different from what I experienced.

That recent walk alone back to the old farm place filled me with thoughts of the blessings of good girlfriends throughout my youth. The awakening of respect and admiration for Beth Ann and Martha broadened to include others, such as Marilyn and Marilyn, Jane, Janice, Vicky, Nancy, Donna, Ann, Terri, Diane, Gwenda, Debbie, and Joyce.

Conversations and giggles echo in my mind.

TAKING A WALK IN GRANDMA'S GARDEN
Anne

"Yoo Hoo! Grandma?" Poking my eight-year-old head into Grandma and Grandpa Flanagan's house, I yell out my usual greeting. Today is a warm, blue-sky, May day, and I decide to stop by to say "Hi" on my way home from school before I trudge up steep West Victoria Hill. Although Mom encouraged us to stop by our grandparents' house every day, I usually waved to Grandma as she sat at her window, and kept walking with K or Greenie or one of the neighbor kids.

Today, though, I am all by myself and in no hurry. Maybe Grandma has baked fresh rolls or perhaps I can get a few pieces of pink peppermint lozenges.

"Hello, Annie. Please come in," Grandma calls from her kitchen sink. Tall and proper, with her brown hair piled up on her head, Grandma looks kindly over her glasses at me. "How is my little girl? Would you like a warm slice of bread? I just took it out of the oven. How about some butter?" (We all know Grandma uses margarine instead of real butter, but, of course, I happily accept her offer.)

"It's so lovely outside, Annie. Let's take a little walk. Would you like to visit my new pansy bed?"

Nodding yes, with bread in hand, I shyly follow her outside for one of my treasured walks—a stroll through Grandma's garden. For a third grader, Grandma's garden is magical. Throughout Buckhannon, Mary Lois Flanagan has a reputation for having one of the most beautiful, unique gardens in town. As a pastor's wife, she had created flower gardens on small-town parsonage lawns across West Virginia.

Her grand garden at 3 West Victoria, their retirement home, covers most of the small flat front yard and curves around to fill the sloping side yard that adjoins Maxine Thacker's. Skillfully placed rocks allow garden visitors to walk—and granddaughters to hop—through the groupings of brilliant colors and greens.

"Annie, say good afternoon to my new friends," Grandma gently instructs me as I plop on a rock beside her bed of colorful pansies that she has carefully nurtured from seeds over the long winter. Proudly, she leans over to hold a bloom between her fingers as she talks. "See their little smiling faces?" And, stepping from rock to rock, my enchanting afternoon walk with Grandma begins.

Grandma loves each of her flowers and cares for them much like she tended the young girls she counseled during her younger years as a Methodist Deaconess, showering them with attention and respect and encouragement.

My garden walk—two steps forward, one step up or one to the right—holds fading spring delights—daffodils, forsythia, hyacinths, snowdrops. Vibrant blooms of early summer rise up to greet us—peonies, spider plants, pink and yellow yarrow, graveyard moss, early pink roses, white lilies, lambs ear, astilbe. The promising buds of warm summer days appear—roses, daisies, and black-eyed Susans. Even a special wildflower is named for me—Queen Anne's lace.

While the flowers themselves provide sufficient beauty, the striking feature of Grandma's garden—the artistic placement of colors and shapes and sizes and textures—reflects her patient, thoughtful, creative touch.

For an eight-year-old, this garden walk ends much too quickly. Giving Grandma a big hug, I head up the hill toward home. Looking back, I see Grandma bending to pick a purple pansy for Grandpa. This sweet moment lasts forever in my mind's eye.

Peace On Earth

 From "The Wilderness"

MAIN STREET

OUR LITTLE CORNER OF THE WORLD
Greenbrier

Buckhannon is a small town that works. The feel is right. We are like a comfortable sweater or an ol' pickup truck. My friend Mary Ann wrote our town motto: "The promise of tomorrow with the dignity of yesterday." Her father was part-owner of the Ford dealership, and her mother owned the Dairy Queen, both downtown businesses.

My own parents had fallen in love while students at West Virginia Wesleyan College. The college is on one end of Main Street and the hospital is on the other end, just like Colonial Williamsburg, Virginia.

Dad always practiced downtown, first with Dr. Deeds above the Adrian Buckhannon Bank, then on the fourth floor above the Central National Bank. There were very few elevators in town: one in the Barlow Mansion which housed St. Joseph's Hospital, and the other up to Dad's office.

"Flies do not fly above the third floor," Dad explained once, enumerating the reasons to be so high above our Main Street. Certainly the perch at the rounded window proved a great crow's nest from which to watch the annual Strawberry Festival Grand Feature Parade. When Beth was born in 1957, Dad built his little brick office on Kanawha Street just off Main Street.

On Main Street we were blessed with old-fashioned pharmacies. Now burned down, the old Poundstone Drugstore was attached to the Rainbow Restaurant where all our friends gathered for great ice cream floats. Woody Corder, DDS, gave us ten-cent certificates after our dental checkups, redeemable for an ice cream cone at the Rainbow.

We grew up with two shoe stores: Fort Pitt and Rogers. The latter had a working X-ray machine out front where you could not only check your shoe size but also see your metatarsals.

Weekends proved that Buckhannon was a center of commerce, as local farmers and their families descended from all directions on our town. There were hardware and feed store supplies to buy. Visiting took place in front of Murphy's Five and Dime. The crowd was so compacted that a short little fellow like me could hardly walk. Besides that, a great deal of tobacco spitting would be going on, causing me to consider myself a soft target as I attempted to get inside Murphy's to browse the comic books and buy the latest 45 rpm record from the top 10 hit parade.

Liberty Lunch next door sold 10 hot dogs for a dollar. The Lulos brothers kept the place hopping while fomenting political opinion.

Acme Bookstore was perhaps my favorite spot on Main Street. The Oldaker brothers sold magazines and newspapers from across America. They talked sports nonstop. Their offering of sporting goods included baseball mitts, basketballs, and tennis rackets. Every week I'd go in and grab a mitt and baseball, hitting the pocket again and again as I imagined catching that long ball and preventing a home run, winning the game.

Main Street, Buckhannon, West Virginia, satisfied my itch for fun, food, and fantasy as a wild and wonderful mountain burg.

WE WHO RULED
Beth

Let me set the stage by announcing to the world that we, my friends and I, truly believed at the age of 12 years old, that we ruled our town. Chores done and allowance in the pocket, a gang of girls were set loose on the town of Buckhannon. Dinah, Jan, Gini, Jackie, Marti, Luanne—sometimes the names would vary but not the adventure.

Starting at one end of Main Street, we worked our way down, weaving in and out of the clothing stores—The Style Shop, Opal's, Casualaire, the H&P store (who actually knew that meant the "Happy People"?!). Always there was a stop in both Lewis and Anderegg Jewelry Stores to get a charm for our bracelets or order an ID ring for the latest boyfriend (who would, of course, give it back to us to wear, coated in yarn to fit our fingers or on a chain around our necks).

On to the oiled wooden floors of G.C. Murphy's Five and Ten, only cool to stop at the 45 records section and perhaps buy a few cents of candy from the huge selection in the glass cases. The smell of roasting cashews, mingled with the spraying of Midnight in Paris on our bony wrists is the essence of such memories. Oh wait, there was one more dime store aisle to cruise, the lingerie section. With downright amazement and no doubt much scorn, we would pull out the white bras, true brassieres made up of concentric circles, ending with a point. Star Trek bras on Main Street.

Three drug stores, each with a purpose, were our next destination. Bonnie Bell cosmetics lined the old fashioned wooden shelves and beveled glass splendor of Miller's; greeting cards to go through at Thompson's; tempting lipsticks and eye shadows at Poundstone's. How we loved to go into the wooden phone booth inside Miller's and ring the number of the phone booth on the corner of Kanawha and Main, clearly seen out the big plate windows of the pharmacy. We memorized the phone number years before. One time our classmate, who will remain anonymous, happened to be passing on the street when the phone rang. He stopped, looked around, and picked it up. Tentatively, he said, "Hello?" "Oh, M--," one of us said in a ghostly voice.

"This is your guardian angel, coming to let you know we are always here. We are always watching!" We giggled until we were squatted on the floor, trying hard not to wet our pants, as M-- dropped the phone and ran down the sidewalk.

Time now to try on shoes at Fort Pitt and Walkers (I lie not...their real family name), and Luanne's parents' new shoe store. Hush Puppy brand and Aigners were all the rage. One time as we came marching out of the shops, Dinah put her hand up, stopping the troops in our tracks. "Come on, let's follow Bennie and see where he goes." Paying us no mind, the small man (and some may say 'town character') headed toward the A&P grocery store. With complete disdain for hygiene, he blew first one nostril and then the other, flinging "it" into the air with his finger. Did we, the rulers of our town, so much as cringe? Heck no, the gesture now became our new salute, sans the messy mucus, and a parody toward a mean and nasty person, our latest student teacher from the local college.

Back on Main Street, we debated our next adventure. Should we stop for our magazines and comics before or after lunch? The Book Store felt like a place that simply belonged to everyone in town. The clock man stood in front, the lining of his coat filled with watches, opening and closing his jacket like a flasher.

As we pulled out and counted our money, we discussed the merits of hot dogs, french fries and flavored cokes at the Rainbow Restaurant or Liberty Lunch. Or we could have the best pie in town and head down to Maggie's by the railroad tracks. Girls couldn't go into pool halls in those days. The Dairy Queen would be the last stop of the day for a Mr. Misty or a chocolate dipped cone.

Oh, we must remember to run into Home Hardware or Shannon's to get the picture hooks for Gini's mother, our one responsibility for the day. And one of us had won a free makeover at the new Merle Norman store if there was time. Dancing and playing our new records at Jan's house was the promise of the afternoon. Her daddy was the Mayor and her mother ran the town—but, as I said, we knew who really ruled!

STORES TO VISIT
Ruthie

Midday on Saturdays my best friend Marilyn and I would take a walk down the hill, through grass-centered alleys, carefully cross Kanawha Street, and head into town. Main Street during junior-high years had numerous small businesses that could easily occupy the time of a couple of young girls for several hours.

My mother was generous with allowing me to buy new shoes a couple times a year. I would go to both shoe stores to decide which pair was the one I needed. If I forgot the money Mom had given me, I could take the shoes home on approval.

Marilyn and I would head over to GC Murphy's 5&10 Cent Store to look at the fish and hamsters in the back. Then we'd go to the front counter to buy penny candies—either dots of colored candy on a paper strip or a quarter pound of a favorite chocolate.

Next, we would stop into the drug store to test perfume and say "hi," since everyone was gracious to Doc's daughter. Opal's Dress Shop was where my older sister Anne worked, and we might stop in to see the latest arrivals. We were careful not to stay too long and embarrass her.

Main Street had many more stores that captured the interest of small-town girls. One friend's aunt and uncle owned a dry goods store, so a visit to say "hi" to Aunt Lucille and Uncle Tuck was part of the ritual. A walk through both hardware stores and into their household sections gave us ideas about which dishes and casserole plates we would need in our own future homes.

There were shorts and blue jeans to see in the H.P. store, nice new sweaters at Strader's, and even material at Perce Ross for a shirt that Mom might sew for me.

A few favorite places would round out our adventures. First, buy *Seventeen* magazine at the Acme Bookstore. Then we would claim a booth at the Rainbow Restaurant, famished and thirsty from all the walking along those three blocks. We'd meet other girlfriends and hope some of the guys were downtown too. Even if not, a vanilla Coke, an order of French fries, and a dime in the jukebox—or a quarter for three songs—would be the perfect setting for gossip and giggles. There was always something exciting to see or do on Main Street.

SATURDAYS ON MAIN STREET
Anne

Main Street, the vibrant center of Buckhannon in the 1960s, hummed with activity on Saturdays. It seemed that everyone in Upshur County came into town—farmers driving their trucks, families picking out a new chair at the Furniture Mart, housewives shopping at the A&P, Wesleyan College students running errands, and the Almond kids socializing with all our friends.

From the time I was about eight years old, my sister K and I often walked to town together on Saturdays. Usually, we'd have our 25-cent allowance jingling in our pockets and sometimes a whole dollar bill for a new skirt at Gottfried's or material at Perce Ross. On Main Street together, we navigated our way in and out of groups of men standing around talking with a familiar twang, smelling of soap, and chewing their tobacco wads. We sidestepped a spit of brown tobacco juice and watched where we walked to avoid a chaw.

Reflecting back, I am amazed by the freedom Mom gave us. Throughout grade school, K and I roamed the streets of Buckhannon unchaperoned, traveling the half-mile to town by ourselves through the cool city park or a field of tall grass and across busy streets. Once downtown, we made our own choices—good and bad. We selected and purchased shoes and clothes without adult assistance. Mom, who did not enjoy shopping, taught us independence at a young age. Not surprisingly, we developed a carefree, funky style that we still wear today.

Occasionally, Mom drove us downtown to help us deposit college money at the Adrian Buckhannon Bank. What an adventure it was to ride in the big Plymouth with Mom! She was a dreadful driver who jerked along in second gear, causing the car to make loud grinding sounds as she attempted to switch gears. Even with the car noises, we liked going downtown with her because she parked in Dad's office parking lot, and we always ran in to hug Daddy and pick up a red sucker. Lollipop in hand, we scurried up Kanawha Street as fast as we could past the Tap Room where people drank beer.

Often, we helped Dad grocery shop at the A&P, located in

the middle of town. Dad, with Mom's detailed shopping list in hand, gave us assignments to keep us busy. Although the manager may well have shuddered when Dr. Almond entered the store with three or four small children, we never noticed. We happily walked up and down aisles, searching for the cheese or bread, proud of being Dad's little helpers.

About the time I reached junior high, my friends Nancy, Anna Gay, and I met at Janet's house Saturday mornings to put on our makeup before we walked downtown. Once on Main Street, we entered every establishment. We checked out GC Murphy's 5&10 Cent Store comic section, reading a little *Superman* or *Archie* for free, and then conversed with the parakeets. We dashed into Thompson's Drug Store to greet the pharmacists who worked with Dad. We looked longingly at the diamond rings at Lewis' and Anderegg's jewelry stores, and stopped for a minute at Opal's Dress Shop, where I ended up working during my junior and senior years.

After we checked what movies were playing at the Kanawha and Colonial Theatres and made plans to meet up with a big group of friends later that night, we strolled down to the end of Main and stared up at the Upshur County Courthouse, the grandest building in town, and home of the Department of Motor Vehicles. We dreamed of the day we turned 16—old enough to return here for our driver's license. Laughing, we topped off our day with a Mr. Misty at the Dairy Queen and headed toward home.

OUR TOWN
K

Saturday morning and the sun is perking up. My little sister Annie and I decide to go check out "our town." All our chores are done and we have a little change in our eight- and seven-year-old fists. We head for the park to look at all the daffodils in straight rows, a cheery yellow flower on each.

My goal is Murphy's 5 & 10, the little chicks with purple feathers. Or green or pink. I know they will sprout into plain old Rhode Island Reds but how I long for a purple Easter chick. We chat with those chicks for a while.

Let's go up to the Court House then back on the other side, clear down past Kanawha and Spring to Florida Street where the old Post Office is. There's Miller's and Thompson's. Hi! Dr. Howard Thompson with your white coat and your Thompson's Cough Syrup, good for a cough but yucky. Hi! to Eleanor and Joyce! Hi! to Bill Zumbach!

On down the street past Perce Ross Men's Store. And his tiny Women's Store with woolen fabric and socks and Pendleton Suits. There's Strader's, the closest thing to a department store! Across with the red light to the Court House, the grandest building in our Buckhannon world. (Remember ahead to 1960 when Dad packed all of us pajama-clad in the Jeep and took us down to see the Opera House burn? Quite a building. Quite a fire.)

Oh. There's the Rainbow. Cherry Coke as we take possession of the red leather booth. Then on down Main Street. There's Adrian Buckhannon Bank and Opal's and Anderegg's and The Book Store. Hi Joe! Hi Dave! Then comes where Rodgers' Shoe Store went later.

My most memorable moment on Main Street was years earlier when Mom took me and Greenbrier and Annie to visit Maude Hinkle in her big white house with the upper porch. What a fascinating house, the home of a working artist. Bottles full of seeds and lichen and seed pods and dried grasses. And paint. What a luscious smell. What amazing works of art—a big bouquet of lilacs and poppies and roses, all made of her gatherings—and lasting for my lifetime at least. (We have three of Maude Hinkle's works, which remind me of my visit to her home and my love of all things natural.) Wave up, in case Mrs. Hinkle is watching.

On down the street to Gottfried's with Mr. and Mrs. Gottfried and lots of pretty dresses for Easter. Home Hardware with Mr. Herb Stalnaker. And on to Shannon Hardware with Kenny Phillips. We cross the street and stop in at the Post Office. It is a small but lovely old building.

Now comes the new Dairy Queen. Hi Betty Booth! We'll be back. Past the Colonial Theatre and the old A&P (the Atlantic and Pacific I learned later). There's Lewis Jewelers. Hi! Pug and Veda Lewis! And back again to the 5 & 10. Look at all those old guys chewing on their tobacco and spitting on the sidewalk. But I really want to visit my little purple Easter chick one more time.

Annie and I belong to Buckhannon and Buckhannon belongs to us.

THE ROLE OF SPIRITUALITY

YIN YANG CHRISTIANITY
Beth

Although I know very little about the musical group "Twisted Sister," the first time I heard that name I had an "a-ha" moment. I was the twisted sister of the family when it came to religion.

We were raised in a typical 1960s style of expected church attendance, at least in the small-college-town way of central West Virginia. Our church was called First Methodist for a reason; the huge grand building was complete with a stained glass rendition of God's Eye looking down from a high domed skylight. As others prayed and listened to carefully planned and excellently elocuted sermons, my mind wandered to images of swinging from the long light fixtures, working up to a trapeze frenzy, reaching the dome in the center, and perching up there. "What must it be like to be God, looking down on a congregation of the faithful?" And so the questioning took root.

The church of my growing up stressed intellect. My Sunday School teachers were often college professors, many were ordained ministers, and they encouraged long discussions, debates, and the putting aside of church sanctioned lessons for a more stimulating focus on the questions of the day: Is God dead? Who was the historical Jesus? Was the Bible to be taken literally? Was hell a place or right here on earth (as war waged in Viet Nam, civil rights marchers crossed bridges, and a church was blown up in Birmingham, killing little Sunday School children)? Through it all, we sang the hymns of praise, danced the sacred dances, took our pure grape juice communion, and headed off to church camp.

It was at camp that I took those first steps of my yin and yang spiritual journey. I smoked my first cigarettes, but discovered a relationship with the Holy Spirit—both of which have shared my walk throughout this life. Our music became a mixture of the Shaker tune "The Lord of the Dance" and the goose bumps of "One Tin Soldier." The personal relationship with God met the social responsibilities of the day—a handshake that was forever forged in my mind.

Our Youth Group traveled to the Jewish synagogue in another town. Who were these Chosen People of God? Why did the wife of an Indian professor have a dot in the middle of her forehead? Who were these Mormons in town who had such nice families, but believed an Angel gave them personal knowledge of Jesus once living in North America? Why did my Catholic cousin have to wear a hat when she went to her church and crossed herself after the meal-time prayers? And what of this Rapture when saved football players and airline pilots would disappear when Jesus came back in the clouds?

I found solace sitting on rocks in the Wilderness stream, praying and blessedly feeling, sensing, and even hearing the Holy Spirit. "You, Elizabeth, are Loved." I later learned, as I went on to receive a bachelor's degree in Religious Studies, that a theologian named Martin Buber had a name for this relationship with God: "I—Thou." For me, nothing else has mattered. I learned in those early days of childhood that I was loved by a Creator who is personal and present. No matter where or how far I roam.

THEOLOGY OF GRACE
Ruthie

Every weekday evening, promptly at 6 p.m., our Almond family gathered around the oval dining table in our country kitchen and had a meal together.

Our mealtime was an open conversation time. All topics and opinions were encouraged. We children learned to disagree, but were not allowed to be disagreeable. All ages and views were respected.

Those evening meals were reflective of our family's spirituality. We began each meal with a three-part prayer to Christ.

> God is great,
> God is good.
> And we thank Him
> for our food.

The food on the table came from Daddy's hard work to earn a living and his job of doing the grocery shopping. All of us also worked hard to grow the family garden. And Mom canned or froze the harvest of fruits and vegetables for the winter months. But we thanked God for giving us the food because He gave us the talent and energy to work.

> By His hand
> we all are fed.
> Give us, Lord,
> our daily bread.

Our family table was open to many, many visitors. The "all" included any guest whom any of us children had visiting that evening. Or in the summertime it was the cousins who came visiting from New Jersey or Florida or Pittsburgh.

Or the older relatives who became part of our family. People like our grandparents who lived down the road—and Grandma made homemade "daily bread." Or her widower brother, Uncle Paul, who lived in the garage apartment next door to us.

(He was my caretaker until he died when I was in kindergarten.)

"All" included Mrs. Stansberry, who always had Sunday dinner with us. Or, after she passed away, another widow, Janie Lou.

And then there were "all" the dozens of international students who had homestays with our family for short or long visits. One man, named Friday, stayed for over four years. Around that table we discussed various religions, but Mom would come back to those grace words, that it was the Lord Jesus Christ who gave us our daily needs.

> Help us to do
> the things we should,
> to be to others
> kind and good.
> Amen.

Our spiritual learning from that prayer before the meal was backed up by our parents' actions. We saw how they treated others with great kindness. That garage apartment for Uncle Paul later became home for our cousin Kirk during his college days. And for my friend Jane when she was a newlywed before the couple's deployment overseas. And for Bill, who wrote songs. My folks' generosity of sharing meals extended to their generosity of free use of that apartment for various people.

God is good. God provided for our needs. God would help us to also be kind and good to others.

That simple grace prayer helped shape my theology as, day after day, before our meals we acknowledged in our home truths about the one true living God. Through those words.

SPIRITUAL TRUTHS
Anne

When my dear sibs suggested writing about the influence of spirituality in our childhood home, I felt unsure, even anxious. After all, I'm a businesswoman—not a pastor or a missionary or a theology major. I'm more comfortable preparing a balance sheet than writing a paper on spirituality. Outside of church discussions, I've not given the topic much thought. Am I even "spiritual"?

So I've been wondering. What if spirituality is simply the process of seeking a meaningful connection to something bigger than myself? Perhaps spirituality is actually that path of living that allows me to practice the truths my parents taught.

Mom and Dad were what I call foundational Methodists. Their lives, their actions, their family centered around the Methodist Church, and the church served as the spiritual foundation for our family. Growing up, I loved my church—Sunday School, Vacation Bible School, MYF, youth choir—but the rigidity of "church-going" and "church rules" became overwhelming, even suffocating, as I moved into my questioning teens. After I headed to college, I drifted away from organized religion and only returned to the church over a decade later when Richard and I started our family.

During my times of doubt and throughout my life, I found that the spiritual truths Mom and Dad passed along to me were freeing, uplifting, and sustaining. I learned how to live my life by remembering how they lived theirs. They taught us to. . .

Love abundantly. Love your family. Treasure your spouse above all others. Love your friends and neighbors and those who disagree with you. Bring them to your dinner table. Love the earth. Play in a stream. Look at the stars.

Show compassion. Operate from your heart. Treat those who are less fortunate with dignity. Welcome vegetables and venison as valued payment of debt.

Be grateful. Don't be envious of others. Strive to grow and learn and improve, but be content. Happiness comes from taking time to appreciate what you have.

Read. Every day. A book. A poem. A bedtime story.

Take a walk. Every day. For your health. For peace of mind. By yourself or with another. Rejuvenate. Discover.

Plant a garden. Strawberries and raspberries and tomatoes and corn. Lilies and geraniums and daisies.

Work hard. With a dream. With integrity. With passion.

Laugh out loud. Often.

A FIRM FOUNDATION
K

"God is great and God is good." We said that prayer at least twice a day (not over our breakfast orange juice). So I had the sense that God was good, in particular, good and loving toward me.

When I was a baby, I learned that my mother and my father loved me. Because I had a brother a year older and a sister a year younger, I knew that the love for me was not exclusive. I soon sensed that Mom and Dad loved each other too. I was blessed at First United Methodist Church; the first Bible verses I learned were "God is love" and "Jesus went about doing good."

One time a friend said to Mother, "Lois, you have your head in the clouds." Mom smiled. "Yes, perhaps. But I have both feet planted firmly on the ground." I sense that Mom taught me that. Innocent or "filled up with God." But also real, seeing and knowing the sadness and the hurt and the evil of this world. "As innocent as a dove. As wise as a serpent."

God through my family. God through nature. God through the stories of the Bible. God through books that opened new worlds. God through music, especially the old hymns. God through silence, off in a corner of my messy room or off in the crabapple blossoms of The Enchanted Forest. God through work. God through Sunday School and Vacation Bible School. God through community. God through the questions that swam around in my mind and my gut. God through my body as I ventured barefooted to celebrate the first of May, running down to the strawberry patch.

"It's me. It's me. It's me, O Lord. Standing in the need of prayer." Yes, prayer. Yes, need. Yes, me. And God willingly holding out firm hands to me. Under that prayer God was asking me to extend that loving sense to everybody else. "What a friend we have in Jesus."

I am so grateful for a firm foundation, for safety and security, for good theology. Rare and precious. Life has gotten hard. I have known betrayal and fear and meanness and ugliness. I have seen and felt oppression and disease and doubt. Loss is a theme of human life. But underneath are the Everlasting Arms.

As a little child, I was encouraged to ask questions, to look everywhere for answers, to create my own answers out of the stuff of this world, and to keep on asking and growing.

Mentors who guided me in my early years? Mom, Dad, Grandmother, Grandpa (as a shadowy figure who read his Bible and his hymnal and preached up at French Creek), Mrs. Stansberry, Uncle Edward, Dan and Martha Daniels, their daughter Patsy. And then there were my Sunday School teachers: Miss Hartman and Mrs. Smallridge, Mrs. Tetrick, Sue Darnell, Esther O'Brien, Elaine Davis, Betty Weimer, John Warner, Wayland Taylor, Joe Mow, Stanley and Glenadene Martin, and Phyllis Coston. I also learned about life from Greenbrier and Annie, Ruthie and Baby Beth and Brier and all the kids in the neighborhood.

GRANDDAD, THE PREACHER MAN
Greenbrier

Grandfather Flanagan gave us gifts at Christmas and our birthdays of a dollar and a handwritten sermon based on a hymn, all tucked into a *National Geographic* magazine. From his sharing I knew spirituality was important: we consist of Body, Mind, and Spirit.

The dollar went to snacks at the movies or a Saturday morning treat at the Rainbow Restaurant, along with Mom's instruction to give a tithe—a dime—to the church collection.

The *National Geographic* magazine expanded my horizons with pictures and text of faraway places and exotic animals. What a mind expander!

The sermon shaped around a hymn of the church lit my spiritual fire.

Christmas afternoon, 1958, after all my presents were opened and neatly stacked in my room, I lay on my bed by the window, snow blowing outside. I picked up Grandfather's sermon, written with ink sucked up into his pen from a bottle. There were no smudges on the page like my writing had. He used blue ink, not green ink like Dad liked to use.

His choice of hymn used for inspiration was "Hark! The Herald Angels Sing." As I lay there pulling the covers around my body to stay warm, I laughed again at Mom's joke when she saw the hymn:

"Look," she said, "an angel named after Dad, Harold. 'Hark, the herald angel…'"

Mom could be silly sometimes, I thought to myself.

"Glory to the newborn King" let me dream again of our summertime, with morning glories planted along our wooden fence between our road and Pinto Scout's pasture. My little sister Annie picked the first blue flowers of summer, running with a fistful into our home yelling, "Glory! I've got glory! Mom and Dad, I've got glory!" We had all laughed at that time with a special joy. I laughed again remembering. Glory is much more than just a wonderful blue flower that blooms early in the morning, only to close up in the afternoon.

My eyes studied the verse speaking of "peace on earth." Dad

and Grandfather had been talking about that on Veteran's Day, when Grandfather talked of World War I, the war to end all wars. Dad talked of World War II and how it made the world safe for democracy. I really didn't understand what they were saying, but I knew peace, not war, was the way to live. Grandfather wrote of Jesus as the "Prince of Peace."

Mom explained it to us using the word *JOY* as an acronym. She said the way to have peace is to keep Jesus first, others second, and yourself third. *Jesus-Others-You* is *JOY.*

For the third point of his Christmas sermon, Grandfather wrote about angels and angel voices. He liked to hear his grandchildren sing. When we stopped by to make rolls on Saturday mornings and to watch their television set, Grandmother would often ask us to slip down the hall to Grandfather's bedroom, where he would be lying on the bed like I was doing on this Christmas afternoon. He would be reading the *National Geographic* magazine like I was now. He would greet us and chat with us, then ask us to bow our heads and pray with him. Usually Grandfather spoke softly, but when he prayed to God, he spoke loudly and boldly.

I decided to do that too. I bowed my head and prayed loudly: "Thank You, God, for 'Christ is born in Bethlehem! Hark! The herald angels sing, Glory to the newborn King.'"

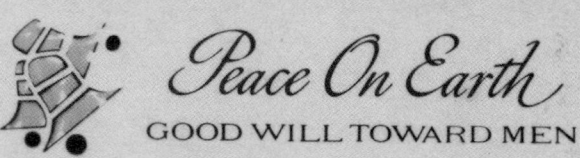

Peace On Earth

GOOD WILL TOWARD MEN

'K', Beth, Ruth, Anne,
Greenbrier, Loie & 'Doc'

MY SIBLING

SISTER BETH
Ruthie

My younger sister, Beth, came into my life when I was four years old. One of my first memories of her is her arrival into the family home. For the rest of our childhood it was the three older kids and the two younger girls. I went from being the youngest of four to being the older of the two younger ones.

Beth was sweet and secure, which gave her a sense of daring. As children, I followed the rules, and Beth quietly broke them. Because she was so likeable, she could and did get away with mischief.

One example is when I got grounded at age 17 for being out too late with my boyfriend, something that had not occurred before. Beth in the meantime, at age 14, was playing with friends, walking into town, or smoking at all hours. But she was like a lovely butterfly that you dare not capture or pin down.

Today, Beth has hundreds of friends, both on Facebook and in the many groups she is a part of in her small town near the Blue Ridge Parkway. There is the Postcard Club, the Wild Women, the Spiritual Group, her church, her work at the Reynolds Homestead, and her two book groups. She has friends from childhood, college, the state she lives in, and Australia— where she spent her senior year of high school. I would not be surprised if many of those people each thought they were her best friend.

Beth has a memory like no one else I know. Not only does she remember all these people, but also events, foods, and books.

Beth reads all the time and remembers all the authors, book plots, and characters in these many books.

She listens to NPR, but never watches TV. She has a strong independent streak in her politics. She is constantly even-keeled and generous. Rarely does Beth say anything bad about anyone else. She is very non-judgmental and accepting of others. She greatly dislikes conflict.

Beth is a combination of the best characteristics of each of our parents.

BIG BROTHER GREENBRIER
Anne

He had the most unusual name in our town, and my big brother owned it. He was proud of it. His matter-of-fact attitude deterred other kids from taunting him. When a new kid asked how he got that name, he'd happily tell the story about his namesake, an old man our parents met when they were on their honeymoon. Surprisingly, most kids and even his teachers didn't know it wasn't even his real name until he went down to the courthouse when he turned 18 to make it legal. He paid a whopping $150— $15 a letter: G-R-E-E-N-B-R-I-E-R. For good measure, he made sure *Greenbrier* came before his birth name *David Ralph*.

Growing up, we fondly shortened Greenbrier's name to *Greenie*. Mom sweetly called him *"Greenbrierie"* when she wanted a favor like getting a log for the kitchen fire. Grandma Flanagan was the only person I ever heard call him *David*.

Greenbrier developed a strong character not only because he had to defend his unique name, but also because he was the older brother of four adorable little sisters. After K and Ruth and I came along, he fervently hoped the next baby would be a brother named Huckleberry Finn. When Beth was born, he was disappointed, but quickly accepted his role to watch over his sisters. The five of us played well together most of the time. We climbed apple trees, played Monopoly in the attic, hit ping pong balls in the basement, and ran through the neighborhood hills. As the oldest, Greenbrier accompanied us to school, to the park, downtown, to the swimming pool, to church, and to Loyal Temperance Legion meetings. When he became the first teenage driver in the family, he taxied us to school activities, piano lessons, friends' homes, and even shopping.

Greenie never met a tree or a stream he didn't like. He loved walking to school, building dams in rain-filled ditches on our curvy dirt road, playing in the yard with his best neighborhood friend, Danny, swimming in the cold Buckhannon River at 4-H Camp, running cross-country, taking long snow hikes with his friend Mike, sledding down Brooks' hill, biking to Spruce Falls in Brushy Fork, camping at the Boy Scout Freezeree, hiking to the top of Mt. Hibbs, and marking the boundary lines at the

Wilderness.

Greenie loved to laugh, and he sang loudly and off-key, especially on vacation trips in the car where he got the prized shotgun seat in the front with Mom and Dad. Oh how the back seat passengers rolled their pretty eyes when he belted out his favorite camp song, "Them Bones Gonna Rise Again."

Curiosity. Greenbrier possessed that character trait in abundance. He would wonder aloud at the dinner table if dreams connect to reality or what makes people smart or why people laugh when they are embarrassed. This curiosity, this wondering about what makes people tick, helped him become a gifted psychiatrist.

Greenbrier had a strong sense of self at an early age. In high school, he excelled in English and public speaking, and was active in the Debate Club, the *Buccaneer* newspaper, Methodist Youth Fellowship, 4-H, the marching band, and he became an Eagle Scout. Once he got to college, he focused all his efforts on his dream of becoming a doctor. He lived at home during his Wesleyan years because, he said, without the distraction of dorm life, he could achieve better grades and increase his odds to get accepted to medical school.

Greenbrier enjoyed a close connection with Mom and Dad. We girls teased him, telling him he was Mama's favorite. And he probably was. Thinking back, Mom formed a tight bond with newborn Greenbrier in Nebraska. They relied on each other while Dad served in Japan. Being the only boy, Greenbrier was Dad's go-to helper. Together, they chopped wood for fires, built bridges at the Wilderness, planted penny Christmas trees, and picked strawberries. Greenbrier and Dad solidified their friendship as medical colleagues. Father and Son developed a mutual admiration and respect during Greenbrier's medical school years and especially when Greenbrier returned to Buckhannon to join Dad's medical practice. Although Dad used to joke that psychiatry was the least-revered medical specialty, he was immensely proud of his son the psychiatrist.

Greenbrier adopted Mom's and Dad's values, their moral compass. He wanted to do things the right way and he tried to behave as our parents expected. Seldom did he get into trouble. Sometimes, though, he acted like a typical teenager.

Rumor has it he often skipped out on church when he was in high school. He and his friend sat up in the balcony above the family pew so Mom and Dad could not see him. After the first hymn, the two of them would walk over to his friend's grandmother's house, which was near the church. There, they would have a snack and talk for 45 minutes, scooting back over to their balcony seats just in time for the final hymn.

Another time, one early Christmas morning when he grew tired of waiting for Mom and Dad to wake up, he started throwing his stocking silver dollars at his sisters. He managed, instead, to hit one of Mom's best green living room lamps. The flying coin sliced a perfect hole in the glass base. We couldn't wait to tattle.

Greenbrier loved growing up in the small town of Buckhannon with school and church activities, the Strawberry Festival, West Virginia Wesleyan, our close-knit neighborhood, and our beloved Wilderness. Like all of us Almonds, Greenbrier is fiercely proud of being a West Virginian. And, he continues to proudly own his distinctive West Virginian name.

MY LITTLE SISTER RUTH
K

Toni Morrison taught me a new word. Actually a word I should have known, but never met. The word in the novel *A Mercy* is *ruth*. It means compassion or mercy or sympathy. I know the word *ruthless*; now I know *ruth*.

My sister Ruth is full of ruth—compassion, mercy, sympathy. She has been that way since the beginning. Overflowing with compassion, a feeling with or for whomsoever was in her path.

Our widowed Uncle Paul lived in the apartment over the garage. He seemed gruff to us three older kids but he loved Ruth so much. They were a separate little universe unto themselves—Ruth was just who Paul needed to cut through his loneliness and Paul was just the babysitter Mom needed and just the adoring friend Ruth needed.

When Uncle Paul died, Ruth was six years old. She felt that loss deeply but she was in kindergarten and was beginning her life-skill of making and nurturing her friends. In Mrs. Reger's kindergarten class, she sat at a table with the A's, the B's, and the C's. Brent Berisford, Mike Campbell, Steve Carter, friends she had all the way through school. Ruth, as an A, was the first graduate of public kindergarten in West Virginia.

Making and tending her friends is Ruth's strength. Along came Marilyn Shissler; Ruth and Marilyn have been lasting friends all these years. Ruth is the one of us Almond kids who reached out most to the country kids. What a rich source of friends. Martha, Beth Ann, Vicki.

As a little girl, Ruthie was a character! She had a way with cameras; she hated photo ops and would stick out her tongue. She pushed her hair behind her ears; they were stand-outs. When we travelled in the car we joked about taking a plug for Ruth. She had to pee and pee and pee—all the way to Charleston, all the way to Pittsburgh, all the way to New York.

In New York City she found her way back from the pharmacy on the corner, back to our hotel, up the elevator, and to our room. She forgot to tell Mom; we were all panicked. Where was our eight-year-old sister? Where could she be? When we finally went back to our room to call the NYPD, there she was, curled up in the hall, taking her nap, not kidnapped at all. Mercy, mercy, mercy!

    Ruth is fearless. Her compassion pushes her forward. Going up to a new person and challenging them to be a friend to this little girl. Bringing home another stray cat. Joining in our kitchen table debates full force. (Her opinion mattered!) Hitch-hiking and catching trains in Sweden, Norway, Switzerland, Italy, and France, trusting her big sis and the Universe. Going off to Poland for 17 years as a missionary, when it was not so safe and not so convenient.

    Ruth could not spell and at times she thought she was not smart. But she is very smart. She is a Serious Soul, sometimes weighted down by the world. She loves to read; she writes letters and notes better than any of us; she writes stories and essays that are from her rich memory and her caring soul; she earned top grades in her Masters from seminary.

    Ruth is a lover and a listener. She is a good wife to Rich, an amazing mother to Joseph and Christopher. She loves God; her faith is alive and growing.

    I remember when Ruth was entering seventh grade. She trusted me with her hair and a pair of scissors. A dreadful mistake! Ruth entered her new world with a sad and sorry hair-do. She forgave me. The hair grew. And her trust of me gradually renewed. But she will not let me close to her hair with scissors. Wise woman!

    Ruth loves cats, especially white cats. She loves cooking, baking bread, driving a car, discovering children's literature, exploring art museums, living the seasons of West Virginia. And she will speak her mind. Just ask her.

    Ruth means mercy or compassion; the opposite of *ruthless*. My sister Ruth is full of ruth, the opposite of ruthless.

ANNIE
Greenbrier

Upshur County Youth Camp in Selbyville has a Brigadoon air about it, coming out of the mountain mist not every 100 years but every year. K, Annie, Ruthie, Bethie, and I attended camp there every summer. One magic moment occurred when I was 14 years old and Annie was 12 years old.

Lights out and time to sleep, guys talked back and forth in Cabin No. 3, as teenagers do. From the upper bunk two rows over, I got a request that gave me pause:

"Tell me about your sister Annie."

"Well," I said without further hesitation, "she keeps a neat house!"

My remark was not supposed to be a joke, but the whole cabin roared with laughter. That was an unexpected response to say the least. Behind the question, as I thought about it, was the obvious observation that Annie had girl-next-door good looks.

"Besides being neat, Annie has creativity," I continued. "She changes her hairstyle every day. It is quite a feat to wear a ponytail with bangs one day, a French twist the next day, followed by pigtail braids the day after."

By junior high, Annie had perfected her role as a middle child. Now I know more about the effects of birth order, but from my upper bunk in Cabin No. 3 on a June evening in Brigadoon, I could say:

"Annie has charm. She can get along readily and well, but she is not a pushover. Annie reads Mom and Dad the best of all us kids. She can figure out what to say to get our parents to say yes."

I recounted the time Annie convinced Mom and Dad to take a detour on our family vacation to pass by Ripley's Believe It or Not! Museum in St. Augustine, Florida. Mom wanted to see the Bok Singing Tower in Lake Wales. Dad wanted to get to Miami for his medical meeting. But Annie knew if we left Atlanta and Dad drove our Jeep hard, we could stop to see what we read about every Sunday in the funny papers. Right there with Tarzan and Dick Tracy was "Ripley's Believe It or Not!" column.

"Well, we got there and I loved it. Later we saw the Singing

Tower, and Dad had an exceptional medical meeting. I thank Annie for her charm and her diplomacy."

Lying on the bunk staring up at the ceiling, thinking about what else to tell a room full of teenage boys about my middle sister, I said, "Annie has class. Hey guys, my clothes are simple to say the least. Annie helps me choose to be better. She even taught me how to tie a necktie. She wanted me to have wavy hair, so she curled my blond hair. A bully in junior high started calling me 'Goldilocks' to taunt me. But I did look great with curly hair. I became 'classy' thanks to Annie.

"Annie had our favorite Brier. We always have a dog, and his name is always Brier. My sheep-herding Collie stayed behind in Nebraska when we moved to West Virginia. K's Collie did not prove too friendly, but Annie's 'Brier' is a prince. He even lets us roughhouse with him. He follows us up and down the neighborhood, protecting us from other dogs and even bulls if we get in their pasture.

"Annie takes great care of her Brier. She combs his hair and feeds him table scraps from her plate. Brier knows Annie cares," I declared on that warm night at the Selbyville youth camp. Then I went back to my first thought. "Doggone it, Annie keeps a neat house. If I ever need to find something, Annie knows just where it is. She has Mom's knack for having a place for everything and everything in its place."

I felt fortunate having a little sister like Annie, who proved neat, creative, charming, persuasive, classy, and caring.

SISTER K
Beth

Just a few years ago, I attended a meeting of the Socrates Café, a group of fun thinkers gathered in the back room of a county library in the foothills of the Blue Ridges of Virginia. The question came up, "Who is wise?" After much banter and unable to come to any conclusions, someone suggested we name a person we considered "wise" and see if that shed any light on the question. I quickly spoke up. "My sister, K, is wise." As all the eyes turned to me, I began to describe this woman, born in 1949, the second child of five siblings, eight years my senior. K was always a wise soul.

Gentle by nature, K is curious, determined, a cheerleader for the underdog. Although I don't believe it is imperative in a description of wise, she is also highly intelligent, most likely from the early grades on, the book-smartest of all of us. Learning and a lover of books are my first memories of my older sister. Curled up on the couch under the picture window in the kitchen, K would immerse herself in a book so deeply that she never heard her name being called for supper. Such was her imagination, though not one to be labeled "dreamy." K was a focused child, neat and organized in her work, her person, and her studies.

My memories of K began by the time she was already baking bread for 4-H projects, heading off to summer camps, moistening her clarinet reeds for the junior high band, coming home from the long hike after piano lessons, gently letting me hold the shoes in her extensive glass collection. Add to that a generous nature, a young girl who willingly played the hymns each week for the "Old Men's Bible Class" at church.

It was K who opened my world to many firsts: pizza, mushrooms in spaghetti sauce, picking violets and making syrup for ice cream, a hand-up to climb on the back of our Pinto-pony, walks in the woods to identify wildflowers. The later "firsts" were of a different nature: the music of Neil Young, the writings of the poet Richard Brautigan, staying a weekend in her college apartment, a discovery of her stack of *Ms.* magazines and other feminist writings.

Through it all, K's strength of character and kindness and sense of social justice never wavered. Her path to become a United Methodist minister was surely no surprise. Although shy in her younger days, K seemed to look at adventure as a challenge. She became one of the first of her generation to bop off to Brazil for an exchange summer after learning a few weeks' worth of Portuguese. The next summer, she took a job in rural Webster County, deep in the West Virginia mountains, living in homes still serviced by outhouses and outdoor wells. She headed to Washington, D.C., to voice her concerns over Civil Rights, a questionable war, and inequalities for women. K showed no fear nor hesitation in her student teaching days when sent into the halls of an inner city high school where she was met daily with greetings of "Hey, Ms. Almond-Joy..." She even stayed an extra year beyond the requirement.

K's influence on me was immense, though always subtle. I chose the same college, far away in northwestern Pennsylvania. I was an exchange student to Australia, not nearly as brave to head to a place where I knew no language—something K did many times. She did a stint on a kibbutz in Israel, attended photography school in Denmark, spent a semester of seminary in India, and hitchhiked and Euro-railed across country after country in Europe.

K had and has it all: Determination. Independence. An aura of extreme kindness, but a ramrod back for justice. A lover of literature, of art museums and music and ballet. A humble minister holding the hand of a dying parishioner, a trait learned early in life as she went on calls with our country doctor father.

Surely these add up to a picture of a wise person—one who laughs, learns, teaches, gives, appreciates, prays, writes, and reaches out to others with an eye toward justice—and walks humbly with her Creator.

WEST VIRGINIA

WEST VIRGINIAN—THAT'S WHO I AM
Anne

Our parents' love for West Virginia was contagious. Loudly singing "Oh The West Virginia Hills" together and off key as the seven of us traveled the curvy Selbyville road to 4-H camp, we were proud and happy to be West Virginians.

Dad, born and raised in New Jersey, adopted West Virginia as his home when he attended Wesleyan College in 1939. His affection for our state deepened when he met Mom, who had grown up 40 miles away in Salem. Taking frequent long hikes together, Red and Lois soon fell in love with the Upshur County hills and with each other. In 1949, they returned to Buckhannon to start Dad's medical practice and raise a family, building their little garage house on a favorite hiking spot—a lovely knoll near Mount Hibbs with a view of the quiet downtown valley.

It was not surprising that Mom and Dad passed along their love of our state to us kids. We tromped through forests, played in creeks, breathed the fresh air, dug in the rich dirt. The hills were our playground. Even today, I feel most alive standing on a mountaintop, listening to a brook, walking along a path or planting a sapling in the gritty dirt.

Through the years, Mom and Dad strengthened our appreciation for our state by exploring West Virginia state parks and forests. Typical of the 1960s, we stopped by the roadside at a lone picnic table, brought out white bread and bologna, and slurped cold water from a natural spring as we listened to Dad's history lesson about our destination—Blackwater Falls, Seneca Rocks or Upshur Mountain.

In the late fall of 1961, we traveled to Spruce Knob, West Virginia's highest point at 4860 feet. Starting out on a mild, sunny day, we had no way of knowing that a cold, biting wind would greet us. Slowly circling the mountain road, we reached the top of Spruce Knob. It was a lonely, desolate spot—no cars, no visitors—just cold wind, one-sided spruce trees, and a large rock pile with a big stick in the middle that signaled the highest point. Dad asked us kids to climb the rocks so he could take a picture. We girls wrapped sweaters around our heads to keep our ears warm. That picture of us perched on our state's highest point made a lasting memory as our Christmas card that year.

On special occasions, we'd pack our entire family tightly into Dad's little Willys Jeep and drive 22 miles to the Wilderness, our favorite West Virginia spot. Dad usually had a project in mind—cleaning brush or building a bridge or transplanting a tree. After work, we'd hike the trails, jump from rock to rock in the stream, slide down the waterfalls ruining another pair of shorts, throw stones in the rutty road, and eat dinner around our roaring fire. All seven of us loved having a full day to work and play together as a family.

Fittingly, the Almond Family designated West Virginia Day the most important holiday of the summer. In honor of its importance, Dad declared June 20th as a day off work. Early in the morning, he walked down the hallway to the kitchen in his white t-shirt and green garden pants and said, "Top of the morning! Who wants to help put up the flag?" (If Grandkids were around, he always prefaced that statement with "Little Fellar.") The volunteer scampered to the basement for the flagpole, and Mom retrieved the folded flag from the hall closet. The rest of us ran outside with Dad to the front yard to remove the smooth rock covering a deep hole. We hoisted the American flag as Mom proudly snapped a picture of this significant event.

Besides raising the flag, our other West Virginia Day traditions were simple but precious. We anticipated spending time in the garden with Dad since he had a whole uninterrupted day off. He might request help weeding or picking berries or shelling peas. Then, we played in the yard before starting our family backyard picnic. We cooked hotdogs on the funny-looking but functional brick and cement fireplace that Dad and his friend Charlie Beer had built many years before, ate watermelon for dessert, conducted seed-spitting contests in the twilight, and caught fireflies when it got really dark.

Thinking back to our West Virginia Day celebrations and to the strong love our parents felt for our state, I understand that what happens in our childhood shapes us and makes us who we are. Though my restless, curious 17-year-old self left Buckhannon many years ago, my roots started their growth in the rich, dark soil of West Virginia. Wherever I live, my roots will always be West Virginian. That's who I am.

MY HOME IN THE HILLS
K

Mom was a naturalist who knew and loved the wild-flowers, the birds, the trees of West Virginia. Dad was a naturalized citizen who gave his heart to West Virginia when he first came to Wesleyan College from Millburn, New Jersey, right near Newark and New York City. Mom and Dad gave their love of West Virginia as a gift to us.

Dad invited each of us to go on calls with him; we saw every kind of house and shack and lean-to in Upshur County, and we felt Dad's deep respect for his patients. Annie and I worked in Dad's office and learned more of these folks Dad served. Some interesting characters!

Every time we crossed the state line after visits to cousins in Pittsburgh or New Jersey, we would break out into "Oh the hills, beautiful hills. How I love those West Virginia hills." Later when Ruth and Rich and their two sons were coming home, they sang out "The West Virginia Hills." Six-year-old Christopher declared, "Now I feel real."

Wendell Berry, one of my favorite Appalachian writers, says that many people are "displaced" but he has a different situation. He is "placed." Yes, I was placed from the very beginning and that has given me great freedom. I have loved living in Cleveland, in Boston, in New York City. I have loved travelling all over Europe, India, Brazil and Russia. That freedom to go and explore comes from knowing my place, my home among the hills.

Mom was our 4-H leader. 4-H built pride with songs and stories and camp projects. My favorite 4-H project was West Virginia Trees. How I love the sycamore and spruce and oak and redbud.

Public school gave an emphasis to West Virginia, two full years of West Virginia history, the Golden Horseshoe Award, and for me in sixth grade, the singing of "The West Virginia Hills" every morning just before the Pledge of Allegiance to the flag.

The hills formed all of us here in this place. Row after scattered row of lumps of earth, blanketed with such life. Hard to travel up and down and through the rhododendron thickets. Hard to get from one hollow to the next. Hard to be neighborly when roads were almost impossible and rivers were wild and fickle. This just suited the Scotch-Irish who settled here. Isolated. Independent. Making do. Creative and honest and hard-working with wry humor. Also shy and backward and gullible when the lumber barons and coal barons and gas barons came along with "special deals."

While settling on some of the richest real estate in the world, West Virginians became Poor. West Virginians have been Had so often, we seem defeated. Oppressed. West Virginia now is 49th or 50th in ways that matter. Number of drop-outs. Number of teen pregnancies. Number of meth labs. Number of guns per person. Number of kids who fight and die in all our wars.

Because I started with such love of my place and because I was eager to learn the real stories (thank you, Marvin Carr and Mary Lee Daugherty), I learned about how colonies worked and about exploitation of resources and about the use and abuse of stereotypes. I refused to feel Put Down. I felt righteously defensive and feisty and more and more in love with this place that has formed me, my home.

"MOUNTAINEERS ARE ALWAYS FREE"
Greenbrier

Our West Virginia State Motto says it all: "Mountaineers Are Always Free."

Celebrating West Virginia Day each June 20th, with our Centennial Year in 1963 when I was 15 years old, gave plenty of chances for "Montani Semper Liberi" to sink in.

Helping Dad display the United States flag for multiple holidays, including West Virginia Day, lent weight to the concept of being free. I realized that I am part of something bigger than myself. Joy and contentment came from pledging allegiance to "Old Glory." The joy was complete when I declared, "Mountaineers are always free."

My concept of being free evolved. At first I focused on the idea of free as in no cost, or a bargain. Dad took us grocery shopping at the A&P Grocery Store on Spring Street in downtown Buckhannon, across from the Coca-Cola Bottling Plant. We had Mom's list of food and supplies to purchase, and Dad would have us look for special deals, such as Ann Page store labels. What fun to imagine that Dr. Basil Page's daughter, also named Ann Page, had a bargain for us. Dad would often assist Dr. Page in surgical cases from gall bladders to hernias. Dad loved his coffee. I remember grinding the coffee beans right on the spot. The aroma of fresh coffee would waft through the air as I held the red bag under the grinder.

Another way I began to appreciate being free came from the custom in our home of constantly reading. We would sit together in the sunny summer kitchen, or around the kitchen fireplace in winter, relishing our time of reading. Dad especially liked the *West Virginia Hillbilly*. He would read out loud from the back page column titled "The Comstock Lode." Editor Jim Comstock certainly served up rare gold nuggets of folklore. He billed it as a "weakly" newspaper, but I saw that being a Mountaineer or hillbilly means a lot of things, but never being weak. The good-natured joking often explored our stubborn streak and our passion for independence. Our role models wearing buckskin grew to fit me. I idealized Davy Crockett, "King of the Wild Frontier," from the first grade on after Walt Disney released a popular movie and song about him. How special to sing about being "born on a mountain top. . . in the home of the free." Receiving a birthday gift of a coonskin cap, which I wore proudly on house calls, helped me match Dad, who wore a Russian fur hat in the unheated Willys Jeep. I felt proud to be a Mountaineer.

The Latin phrase for "always"—*semper*—grew to have special meaning the year our family drove to Rainelle, West Virginia to visit the United Methodist Church, built entirely of chestnut lumber, where Mom and Dad married on June 11, 1945. Grandfather Rev. Paul L. Flanagan conducted the service, and Grandfather Henry David Almond came by railroad from New Jersey to witness the union, when they promised to always be true to their vows.

Another type of nut tree—the walnut—and the promise of fidelity became connected for me. One cove near our hilltop home, where we built a winter shed for our horse Pinto Scout, was planted by Mom and Dad with Black Walnut trees. They prized these trees for the promise of future harvest. Grandmother Mary Flanagan prized the wood's dirt she had me gather for her flower garden from under the walnut grove. Her wonderful pansies with their smiling faces added to my joy. Each fall the trees faithfully blessed us with an abundance of walnuts, which blackened our hands as we opened the shells and led us to a reward of 4-H recipe walnut fudge.

Just to think about growing up someplace else makes me shudder. How wonderful to be a West Virginian, where "Mountaineers Are Always Free"! The Almond children have a proud, freedom-loving, promise-keeping heritage honoring our hillbilly home, nestled in the Appalachian Mountains of the United States of America.

THREE DEGREES OF SEPARATION
Beth

Recently a co-worker down here where I work in Virginia came into my office and asked, "How is that if there is a roomful of fifty strangers, the two West Virginians always find each other?" I laughed and acknowledged this happened repeatedly in my life, across the many states where I have lived and traveled. "I'll tell you what else is true," I said to this young woman. "You know how folks talk about Six Degrees of Separation, meaning when talking to anyone in the world, within just six people, we will discover a common person known to both of us? Well, in West Virginia, it seems to only be Three Degrees of Separation—and Two if we're Methodists!"

Although spoken in jest, there does seem to be some common denominator in folks who hail from the Mountain State. Formed out of Virginia in 1863 in the midst of the Civil War, West Virginia had a rough and stormy birth. "West, by God, Virginia" became a rallying cry, a source of pride for a mountain people who had been a bit of an afterthought to the government in far-off Richmond. We were now independent, in charge of ourselves, and, alas, poor.

Surely to a fault, West Virginians were a trusting people, believing that others were as honorable as themselves. "Money for what's under my land? Well sure, I'll take much needed cash. Who wouldn't? Won't hurt a thing." "You want to cut my trees up and down the hills and down to the river? Heck, they'll grow back." And so it began. Outsiders were making vast sums of money from coal, timber, gas, and oil, while the workers and landowners often barely eked out a living. A state stripped almost 100% of virgin forests led to massive flooding. Pockets of communities thrived while others floundered. But through it all was a pervading and immense sense of pride.

West Virginia is called the "Mountain State" because of the rugged chain of the Appalachians that cover nearly every part of our state. Deep valleys, hidden hollers, twisting rivers, mountain tops, huge rock formations, formidable winters, country roads—all of this created many isolated communities.

There were, though, several things that started to bind the

citizens together: unions, church affiliations, the government in Charleston, an early and exceptional state park system, a statewide 4-H program and state camp, two strong universities and a number of state colleges, the Golden Horseshoe contest taken by students after a mandatory year of West Virginia History, the teaching of school kids to learn all 55 counties and their county seats, the railroads that crossed the entire state, and, regrettably, a prejudice by outsiders to decry the West Virginian as a lazy, ignorant, dirt-poor Hillbilly. That stereotype seemed a blanket labeling of all West Virginians, no matter who, what, or where.

Outside of the state, West Virginians learned to honk and wave at cars with West Virginia license plates, formed West Virginia clubs in far-off places, subscribed to proud periodicals, such as the *West Virginia Hillbilly* newspaper or *Golden Seal* or *Wonderful, West Virginia* magazines. A natural friendliness and "where might you be from" is one of the first questions a West Virginian will ask of a stranger. Our unique accents and Appalachian cadence of speech is often easily recognizable to each other. We grew up singing "The West Virginia Hills," could identify our state bird, knew the state motto "Mountaineers are Always Free," and, in later generations, tear up when the song "Country Roads" came over the radio.

What did West Virginia do in forming me, a daughter of its mountains? It made me sometimes more trusting than wise. It turned me into a romantic whose knees grow weak at the cry of a distant train whistle. As I roam the world and stretch my wings and spirit, a small part of my heart and soul always yearns for a rest along a gurgling stream, the taste of sassafras, the smell of clean mountain air, the glory of rhododendrons in bloom, and the figurative bear hugs of our mountain ridges. I do wonder if all West Virginians have that yearning in their eyes and that, indeed, is how we so quickly discover each other in that crowded room.

WEST VIRGINIA INSIDE
Ruthie

I live in Orlando, Florida. My husband, our two sons and I have been in Florida for more than 18 years. Before that, we lived overseas. I have never owned a house in West Virginia, but that is where I grew up.

Homesick. I am always longing for West Virginia. I have not lived in the state since graduating from college, but I consider it home.

I was reading a short story our son Chris Wiewiora published, which included a little bit of his bio. He wrote that he was born in West Virginia. I knew that, of course, since I birthed him there. I still felt a pride and sensed how glad I was I had given his brother and him that gift. We are West Virginians.

What does that mean? I haven't lived in West Virginia since 1976. More than half my life I have lived overseas or in Florida. Why do I have such a pull to West Virginia?

West Virginia shaped my sense of identity. The state is full of nature and low in population. The mountain ridges go on and on in rugged beauty, whether covered in foggy mist, green trees of summer, winter snow or spring colors. In those hills are black bears, wild flowers, and fresh streams and rivers.

The freedom to explore my state as a youth gave me a sense of adventure. Respect for the environment is a core value of West Virginians.

In Orlando, the population is still growing. Developers cut down acres of trees and native shrubs as they plant new subdivisions with houses close together and manicured lawns on weekly watering schedules. The lights shine all night. The airplane and traffic noise is endless. Why does my soul suffer for the homeless animals, no trees for birds, the busy people and strip malls everywhere? I miss the restfulness of slow-paced West Virginia with its quiet sounds of chirping birds, evening crickets and distant coal train whistles.

West Virginia gives me time to think, to ponder, to be. People work hard in my state, but also take time to know each other. Respect for each other's talents is ingrained. Collectively, we West Virginians know how to make quality crafts such as quilts, maple syrup and homemade bread. We produce more than our share of writers, poets, caring medical professionals, teachers, farmers, musicians, artists, lawyers and preachers. We know how to respect each other as well as the land.

This respect for others is another core value inside of me from West Virginia. We talk to each other and ask questions. Curiosity is encouraged.

West Virginia is full of storytellers. West Virginians who have wandered away will find others also from West Virginia and right away seem related. We will understand each other. We will share stories. Often we will both know people in common.

For example, a couple at my church in Orlando and I had the same youth mentor at church camp. An employee at an estate sale saw my Marshall University alumni sticker on my minivan, and we conversed for several minutes, sharing tales of Huntington. A woman in my church Bible study is retired from the FBI facility in Fairmont.

Our son Chris is married to Lauren. They met in Orlando and later moved to Iowa. They have much in common, not least of which is her family background of West Virginia. They did not know that when they started dating, but I think it is part of the magnet that we from West Virginia have with each other. We understand each other in a way that is out of step with the outside world.

MISCELLANY

BOOK BINDING
Greenbrier

Mom reading nursery rhymes to us kids from the orange *Childcraft* book is an enduring memory. Her reading time proved a most cognitively important part of our day. Even now the color illustrations of Jack and Jill climbing the hill and Little Miss Muffet sitting on a tuffet with a spider dangling down beside her come easily to my mind.

Mom read to us at different times, though most often after baths and before nap time in the afternoons. Giving up nap time in the first grade is my only negative memory of starting school. K, Anne, and I would snuggle close, turning the pages of our books. Mother called us "Mexican jumping beans," as we were a rowdy bunch, not being as physically quiet as we should before a nap. One nursery rhyme was about a grandfather who stood on his head. Of course we had to stand on our heads as well.

Mom read in a different voice than the one she used for normal conversation. Later I recognized it as a schoolteacher's voice. At times, Mom would be overly dramatic. I hated it when she read about what little girls are made of—sugar and spice and all things nice—compared to what little boys are made of—snips and snails and puppy dog tails. She made a big deal about it. Gradually I came to realize that I could strategize and win the teasing battle. I could read the words myself, creating my own emphasis.

"What are *little* girls made of?" This would be my way of teasing back.

K picked up reading early, knowing the words and phrases by heart. Anne loved to snuggle and did not try to compete with K and me. When Ruthie entered the family reading circle, I was pressed to the edge. My preference was to climb up on the back of the couch and look over Mom's shoulder.

Later on still, Beth joined our family when I was nine-and-a-half years old. Mom proved a genius at bonding me to Beth. First she was sure that Beth smiled at me first. I was not so sure, but I came to enjoy that distinction. Some evenings before supper, Mom had me read to Beth in the kitchen as Mom prepared the food. I pointed out the words and the pictures, pretending to be a schoolteacher. I always read from the first volume of the *Childcraft* series. I discovered other volumes of the series but never really liked them, preferring to stick to Humpty Dumpty and my other early imaginary friends. Mom did a great job of fostering our imaginations by encouraging reading. Thank you, Mom!

FOUR-LEAF CLOVER
Greenbrier

Mom had eyes in the back of her head when the time came to determine if I was getting into trouble. Maybe her eyes and ears worked together. If she noted that I got too quiet, she'd check on me, as she figured I was hatching some scheme.

Mom's visual acuity was simply phenomenal! Spotting four-leaf clovers in the front yard was one of Mom's favorite pastimes. She could see them while walking across the dewy lawn to check the mailbox after the mailman dropped off the morning letters. Just as a matter of course, she'd gracefully swoop down on a clover patch and come up with a large four-leaf clover. In one afternoon, Mom collected 50 four-leaf clovers so that each and every member of the Upshurite 4-H Club could have one as we pledged our heads to clearer thinking, our hearts to greater loyalty, our hands to larger service, and our health to better living. Once Mom determined we all should have a four-leaf clover, she went about picking them with military precision.

"Keep your eyes peeled," she'd declare, challenging me to keep up with her. While we picked four-leaf clovers, we sang the Depression-era song "I'm Looking Over a Four-Leaf Clover." Mom tried to teach me to find them, but I never had the knack she had. To improve my visual skills, she'd have me read the newspaper upside down. Mom explained that one never knew when a secret clue might be discovered with that inverted glimpse.

Another time we were picking Crimson Clover for the supper table arrangement when we overheard a rather stern and prissy lady comment, "All that Lois Almond does is play with her children!" After holding our breath and our giggles inside for a decent time until Miss Sourpuss was out of sight, we laughed and laughed until we were falling down and rolling in the clover.

Luck of the Irish—that is what Lois Flanagan Almond had in wonderful abundance. Glory be! I'm happy the Almond children had full measure, pressed down and overflowing.

HOPPING DOWN THE BUNNY TRAIL
Greenbrier

Forget about the birds and the bees. When the time came for my talk with Dad about where babies come from, he took another approach.

I told Dad up front that I did not believe a stork brings babies, even though he often told us bedtime stories about Brer Stork bringing a baby down the chimney and putting the baby in the cradle next to the fireplace.

I knew a big baby was too big for a bird to carry in his beak. Besides, Mom had let me feel her belly when the baby began to kick. I was ten years old, and I knew a thing or two. Somehow the baby was inside Mom and was growing more active every day. Mom said she was pregnant, and we would have a baby soon. All summer as Uncle Walter, Cousin Sonny, Cousin Danny, and Cousin Jimmy built Dad's new office at 27 South Kanawha Street, I could see that Mom needed more help with supper. The carpenters really ate a lot after a hard day's work.

My best friend Danny did not know where babies come from either, but he hoped the new baby would be a "firecracker," born on the Fourth of July. Danny and I hoped the baby would be a boy. He had an older sister, Patsy, and I had three younger sisters: K, Anne, and Ruthie. We voted for a boy to help us balance our seesaw view of boys versus girls.

"Okay," Dad said, "let's go look at our rabbits in the cage in the backyard. There is a boy rabbit that we call 'Pete' and a girl rabbit that we call 'RePeat.' That tells us something," Dad chuckled. "We can have a new litter of rabbits after about 30 days. What the rabbits do to make baby rabbits is what married moms and dads do to make babies.

"Remember the eggs from Aunt Lena's hen house?" Dad continued, getting into his story. "Sometimes at breakfast when Mom cracks an egg, we have blood in the egg. Then Mom will tell me we will not eat that egg because it has been fertilized. That is what happens with rabbits, too, though it is not like the Easter Rabbit bringing eggs on Easter morning that we hunt for in City Park, just down across the meadow. There we see the Buckhannon Lions Club walking around the meadow before the hunt begins to see if the Easter Rabbit has brought his eggs."

"Yeah, I know," I said. "Danny and I sneak down and climb an apple tree so we can spy on the Lions," I told Dad, giving away a secret.

"Upon my word," Dad said, picking up on Aunt Lena's phrase, "you and Danny are sure curious.

"Let's just say that the boy bunny is the father and the girl bunny is the mother," Dad went on, "just like the preacher read from the Bible that a man and a woman join together and become one. How God does this is a mystery and a tale for another day."

Just then, Mom called to Dad to say she needed his help. She was in labor. I just knew this was going to mess up Danny's birthday party which was that day, July 15th. Grandmother walked up the hill by City Park to care for us while Dad took Mom to St. Joseph's Hospital.

"Jesus loves the little children…" Grandmother sang.

Later on, Dad came home from the hospital, excited to tell us we had a new sister named Beth and that she was healthy and Mom was doing fine.

I ran up to tell Danny that I had a new sister. He was fit to be tied—a girl born on his birthday!

WHERE THE RHODODENDRONS GROW
Greenbrier

Mom loved wild flowers. When strip mining of coal began, she was "agin' it" simply because the valley fill smothered rhododendrons and robbed the wild flowers of their rich, loamy soil—plain and simple!

To walk a mountain trail with Mom was like hiking up through our hilltop neighborhood, greeting neighbors as they rested on their porches. We greeted each wild flower by name as we paused and chatted a spell.

"Miss Trillium, how good to see you no longer covered by winter's snow!"

"Miss Violet, how nice to see you in your Easter garb!"

"Miss Mayflower, look at all those May Apples peeking out from under your green umbrella!"

"Why, Miss Dandelion, you are already preparing for a spring breeze to carry your babies far and wide!"

And so our hike would go.

When our mountain trail led us to a rhododendron thicket, we just had to enter into the inner sanctum, a sort of Holy of Holies. Inside, protected by an evergreen leafy wall, is where Bambi would seek protection from the storms and from hunters. We could count the deer droppings to determine the deer population.

Inside the canopy of green, Mom would ask us to pause and pray. "Oh God, on the third day of creation, even before you made humans, you made plants. You brought forth vegetation: plants yielding seed of every kind, trees of every kind bearing fruit with the seed in it. And God, you saw that it was good! We thank you for plants of every kind, especially wild flowers. Amen."

After thanking God, we could climb the crooked rhododendron limbs, finding perches extending out over mountain streams running cold and clear. Mom fondly reminded us that humans are not so smart. "They cannot even make soil!" If the brook had silt in it, Mom showed pain the same as I'd feel if I skinned my knee. I hated to see her fret.

One glorious June 20th, West Virginia's birthday, Dad and

Mom took us to the upper reaches of the Buckhannon River to float down in truck inner tubes. Yes, the water was still cold, but the sun shown bright and warm. The word s*pectacular* hardly does justice as a way to describe the rhododendron blooming a light pink from every bough of every shrub. The smiling faces of each flower peered out toward the middle of the dark green river where we laughed, gently floating down our heavenly highway.

Daily my memories can drift back to the mountains where the rhododendrons grow, where the Lord is so near me that when I breathe, He can hear me.

UPON MY WORD
K

Mrs. Stansberry. Neighbor. Friend. Babysitter for the five Almond kids. Creator of Sunday Dinner. As Mom taught Sunday School and joined in worship (especially to meet any strangers and invite them home), Mrs. Stansberry came to our house and fixed fried chicken, mashed potatoes, gravy, green beans, and deviled or beet-pickled eggs. Sunday Dinner. "Upon my word."

Mrs. Stansberry was one of my teachers. She taught me about being a neighbor, about being satisfied, about being rooted. She only finished third grade, up at Hampton. She came at ten years old to help clean the Barlow Home, which later became St. Joseph's Hospital.

She married and settled in, on a small, old farm, up here on Mount Hibbs. Her husband died and she became a young widow, finding her way. When I first made her acquaintance in the early 1950's, she was gray-haired. She looked ancient to us. She had a large garden and chickens, pigs, and a cow. She did a lot of babysitting. She took in foster kids. Gene was her current favorite; she lavished all kinds of TLC on his teen-aged soul.

I did not know then how poor Mrs. Stansberry was. A well in her kitchen. A walk down the honeysuckle path to the outhouse. A bucket of coal beside the fireplace to keep her bones warm. Wheaties for breakfast, lunch, and supper. Breakfast of Champions. But of course she wasn't poor at all, was she? She surely didn't act poor. She had no envy bones, no resentment bones, no dissatisfaction bones. Only a few frustration bones.

I remember her little snap pocketbook with a few quarters and dimes. I remember when Mom would give her the few dollars for babysitting (35 cents an hour was the going rate in the mid-fifties). For every dollar, Mrs. Stansberry would put 90 cents in her purse. Snap. And then she would grab the old cleaned-out honey jar, unseal the lid, and put in ten cents. Tithe. God's money. And she would smile. "Upon my word."

I remember the feeling as a young child of four or five. I would amble up the hill to her old farmhouse and open up the door. "Yoo-hoo." And from deep inside would come her reply. "Yoo-hoo." She would come out, and rock with me on the old porch swing. No one else in my world was that ready and able to be with me. And no one else thought I was such a fascinating kid. I knew Greenie or Annie or neighbors Patsy or Danny would get the same loving care but I still felt especially welcomed. Mrs. Stansberry would listen to me. She would laugh. "Upon my word."

WHAT I MISS MOST ABOUT CHILDHOOD
K

I remember my Nephew Joseph at seven years, one day in the back seat of the car, asking his Mom plaintively, "Mom, does life get easier?" I swallowed a laugh and looked over at driver Ruth, who always had the grace to treat her children with respect. "No," said Ruth. "I don't think so. But you will get stronger and stronger."

What do I miss most about childhood?

I miss going bare-footed and bare-bottomed and bare-all-over out in the grass.

I miss being innocent, though I am still of that ilk.

I miss the nerve I had to eat unwashed veggies from the garden—peas and potatoes and home-grown tomatoes. And the nerve to trudge through poison ivy and greenbrier patches, climb over barbed wire fences and walk serenely through The Enchanted Forest, dark and still and a little formidable.

I miss my Mom and Dad and the security of their presence.

I miss the endless day. Head home when the sun goes down at 8:30 or so in the summer—but that is hours and hours and hours away.

Summer melts into autumn. Autumn becomes winter. I am now in my mid-60's. I have finally grown a little stronger.

HEY DAD!
K

Hey Dad! Hey Doc!
    You had enough signatures to make you a town character.

Green tie. Green ink. Green Jeep.

Collie dogs named Brier.
    "You dog of a dog."

Wesleyan dollars. Two-dollar bills in the offering plate
    and for birthdays.

Coffee in <u>the</u> mug.

The flag up every 4th of July and WV Day and even Christmas.

Strawberries. Blueberries. Strawberries. Raspberries.
    Strawberries.

Yellow roses. Digitalis. Serviceberry.
    Forsythia and pussy willow forced in the spring.
    Crimson clover. A fistful of early spring violets for Mom.

Oh yes, The Chief. Sugar. Loie. Beloved.

But first the little redhead with his sisters and brothers.
    "All born with library cards in their mouths."
    Richard and Ralph. Dot and Mil and Grace.

New Jersey. Millburn. Maplewood.
Scouts. Sunday School. Violin lessons. Caddying.
    Appalachian Trail.
    Fire tower in Vermont.

Then off to Wesleyan, doctor-dream surging.
    My home among the hills.
    "I wasn't born in West Virginia

but I got here just as soon as I could."

Long walks with Lois Flanagan.
    Yes, this place up near Mount Hibbs, near Lena Stansberry.
    Yes, five kids. A house becoming a home. Dreams.

Medical school. Chicago.
    Army. Nebraska. Japan.
And home again.

"What I wanted most was the opportunity to practice medicine."
And so he did.
    12,000 patients. 3,200 births.
        Office open—6 mornings, 3 nights—
            Come flood or blizzard or mud or ice.
        One week off for the AMA meeting.
    St. Joseph's Hospital. The ER begun.
        Week by week by week. Year by year by year.

Making a living. Making a life.

40 years of doctoring with house calls in the hills.
    Helvetia. Pickens. Hemlock. Get Out.
    Hacker Valley. Volga. Ellamore.

Medical detective. Diagnostician.
    List of 10 Most Wanted Diseases. Always on the lookout.
    Medicine as a science and an art.
    Stories of a West Virginia Doctor.

Making a living. Making a life.

Sunday in the same pew at First United Methodist.

The Wilderness. Scouts. 4-H.
    Selbyville with its new swimming pool.

Heroes: Perry Mason. Douglas MacArthur. Nicholas Hyma.
    Doc Cunningham.

Friendships: Charlie Beer. Raymond Lockwood. Russell Westfall. Dick Ralston. Dan Daniel. Jim Comstock. Basil Page. Jake Huffman. Bob Chamberlain.

Advice to his children: Go to school. Keep going. Learn to swim. Save money. Pay your debts.

Storyteller. Gardener. Husband. Father. Grandpa. Doc.

Deep respect for his patients and for most everybody.
    Deep joy at his calling.
        Deep contentment with his life.

Making a living. Making a life.

Stubborn. Honest. Shy.

Free from any need to impress.
    "Here I am. Take me as I am."

Introspection almost nil. An emotional mystery.
    The roots seen only in the fruit.

Hey Dad. Hey Doc.

    The fruit was
        abundant and sweet.

                              written June, 1999
                              for Dad's funeral

LIKE A TREE
K

"Like a tree planted
   by the waters,
      I shall not be moved."

God sends a friend.
   "What metaphor will lead
      you through the cancer?"
   "Are your metaphors in place?"

As if asking if the hats and scarves
   are in my Grandmother's big blue basket
      ready to top my hairless head.

   I ponder the red poisons
      I will let into my veins.

   I ponder the fatigue, nausea,
      dimness of wit, infections,
         complications yet unnamed.
   I plan to be well but I do ponder.

   I look out my window.
      Wind moving mightily through the grove.
         A rush, a heave, a shudder, a sigh.
      No trees crash, not today.

The three spruce marking Childhood Christmases
   by the driveway
   by the bend in the road
   by Mother's garden.
Thom's apple trees.
The 4-H oak of my brother, my 4-H maple.
The new chestnuts willing off the blight, for today.

Planted by the waters. Moving but unmoved.

With Luther I would hope to say,
    "If I knew I would die tomorrow,
        I would plant an apple tree."

With Tillich I might declare,
    "If I were not a Christian
        I would be a tree-worshipper."

With theologian Johnny Appleseed I would say not a word,
    but plant that word
        again and again across the wilderness called cancer.

                              Summer 2006

REALLY SICK
Anne

Her small body huddles on the bed in the corner of an antiseptic-looking room. The morning light shines through the single window onto the pea-green walls.

When she opens her eyes, the room looks blurry. Where is she? Why is she lying inside a large plastic tent? Why can't she move her legs? What are those large shiny rods hanging from the top of the tent, thrust into her tiny legs, pinning her down?

Scared. Puzzled. Only three years old and all alone. Tears roll down her face.

She whimpers, "Mommy. Daddy. Where are you?" Then she calls more loudly, "Mommy! Daddy!"

Through the blurry tent, she sees the door to the room open. Two women rush to her bedside. Both smile. They unzip the tent so she can see them clearly now. A tall young woman in a white dress and an odd white hat asks her how she feels this morning. Tearfully, she gulps and answers politely as she has been taught, "Fine. Thank you." And then she can't help but add, "I want my Mommy."

The other woman, dressed all in black, kindly tells her that she is in St. Joseph's Hospital and that her Daddy is down the hall but he is coming right away. This answer makes her feel better. She's been in the hospital with Daddy before. This is where he works. He helps sick people get well.

Remembering her hospital visits with Daddy, she asks the woman in the white dress, "Are you a Nurse?" And to the other woman with the twinkling eyes, "Are you a Sister?" Both women smile and say yes. Emboldened by her good memory, she looks at the Sister, "But you don't look like my sister K." The Catholic Nun laughs out loud.

Suddenly the door swings open, loudly banging against the wall. Daddy runs over to her bed, reaches through the unzipped tent and, with a cry of joy, gives her a big hug. "Oh, Annie, I thought we had lost you."

Surprised by all the attention and her Daddy's misty eyes, she shyly asks, "Daddy, why am I in the hosbiddle? Where are Mommy and K and Ruth and Greenbrier? Why did you build this tent for me?"

Patiently, Dad explains that she has been very sick. "Three days ago, you told Mother that you didn't feel well. You had a very high fever and had trouble breathing. We put you in the car and drove here as fast as we could. The nurses put this tent around you so you could breathe more easily. It's called an oxygen tent. Since you feel so much better this morning, I think we can take the tent down later today. Right now, I want you to try to take a nap while I go home and get Mother."

Satisfied, she starts to close her eyes, but then the tears come again. "Daddy, what's wrong with my legs? They hurt and I can't move them."

Her Daddy's face clouds over as he answers thoughtfully. "Honey, we had to put i.v. needles in your legs so the hospital could feed you and give you medicine. You were too sick to eat anything."

"Daddy, I can eat now. I promise I'll eat my meals. Please take the needles out. Please."

"OK, honey. I will." Her father shifts into doctor mode, asking the nurse to find Dr. Huffman. Within the hour, the two doctors and a nurse swiftly, yet painfully, remove the i.v. needles from the three-year-old's little legs as she cries softly. With the monster needles removed, she sips a delicious cold drink through a straw—the Nurse says it is called lemonade. She then turns on her side and soon falls asleep in her tent.

When she wakes a bit later, talking and laughter fill her room. Mommy unzips her tent and gives her a big smile and then a kiss and a hug. "That's my girl," she whispers.

Greenbrier and K climb up on the bottom of her bed and wave to her through the blurry plastic. Greenbrier soon spies the big cup on her bedside table and helps himself to a large slurp of lemonade. He, too, thinks it is the best drink he has ever had.

K tells her to come home soon so she will have someone to play with. K also makes a big deal of telling her Dad says she and Greenbrier are special. "That's the reason we get to visit our little sister in the hospital even though we are only five and six years old. Do you know you're supposed to be twelve years old to visit someone in the hospital? Isn't it nice to know we are special? We can come here any time to see you." Oh how happy she is to listen to her talkative big sister.

She is even happier when Mommy decides to spend the night with her. Later, lying in the quiet darkness with no tent over her head, she hears Mommy softly breathing in the bed next to hers. She is no longer afraid, and she feels much better. She is excited for morning to arrive. Tomorrow she will be going home.

P-NEUMONIA
Anne

When I was in first grade, I received a powerful gift. Our teacher, Mrs. Strader, told us that we could grow up to do anything we wanted to do. At five years old, I dreamed big. I positively knew I was going to be a veterinarian.

To help us better understand all the job choices we might have when we grew up, Mrs. Strader asked each student to stand in front of the class and tell what kind of work her mother and father did. Like most of the other kids, I said my mother took care of me and my brother and sisters. Then, I proudly said my father was a doctor. After I told the class about him taking care of patients in his office and at the hospital, I said that I had been in the hospital, too.

Almost teasingly, Mrs. Strader asked if I had "helped" my Dad at the hospital.

"No," I answered. "When I was three years old, I was a patient in the hospital." Peggy, my new best friend, raised her hand and asked if I had been in an accident. I excitedly explained. "I was very sick. I had *P-neumonia*." Naturally, I carefully pronounced the *"P"* out loud, just like Daddy always said it.

Immediately, I saw Mrs. Strader put on her isn't-that-cute smile that teachers give students when they've made a humorous mistake. I also heard a giggle from Nick, the smartest kid in the class.

"Don't you mean to say *pneumonia*, Anne?" Mrs. Strader kindly prompted.

"No. The word is *P-neumonia*," I responded boldly, again emphasizing the *"P"* at the beginning. "That's the way my Dad says it, and he's the doctor, and he should know." A little less patiently, Mrs. Strader told me she thought I was mistaken and advised me to ask my Dad that night.

Defiantly, I rushed home after school. I could not wait to talk with Dad at suppertime. He would tell me I was right. As soon as our family sat down at the kitchen table and said our "God is Great" grace, I blurted out, "Daddy. Why was I in the hospital when I was three?" Immediately, Dad answered with a big voice,

"Honey. You had *P-neumonia*." (He pronounced the "*P*" loudly like I had in school.)

When I told Dad and the rest of the family what had happened in class, Dad looked at me a bit sheepishly. He then admitted that Mrs. Strader was correct. The real way to pronounce *pneumonia* was without the "*P*" sound. He said that he was just trying to make the word sound more fun so I would remember it.

Less confidently, I returned to school the next day and shyly told Mrs. Strader that my Dad said he had just been trying to be funny and that she was right.

Not until several years later did I truly understand that certain words have silent letters, but I did learn a valuable lesson about Daddy. Whenever his eyes twinkled as he told a story in his "funny" voice, I would look at him and wonder, "Is that true?"

SIXTH GRADE JITTERS
Anne

In early September, we bid farewell to carefree days of riding Pinto Scout, running barefoot on the grass, playing hide-n-seek and red rover, and catching fireflies in the dark. I'd had a blast at 4-H and Girl Scout Camps and Vacation Bible School, but now it was time to get outfits organized and make plans with friends. It was time for school to start.

On the first day of sixth grade, Greenbrier, K, Ruth, and I argued, as usual, about who took too much time in the bathroom, and we protested when Mom encouraged us to eat a healthy breakfast. I proudly put on my prettiest circle skirt with big puppy faces, the one Mom had sewn for us three older girls when our family took a trip to New York City. It did look fine. Keeping with tradition, we lined up in front of the garage for our annual first-day-of-school picture.

Waving to Bethie who would stay at home with Mom for another year, Ruthie and I headed down our gravel road toward Academy Grade School with neighbors Timmy and David. We tried hard to keep pace with Greenbrier, K, Jeff, and Danny, who were now in Junior High. We enjoyed the quarter-mile walk, talking with each other and kicking pieces of gravel up and down our steep hill. This day, I happily skipped toward school, aiming to arrive before the tardy bell so I could get the new year off to a good start.

Sixth grade was a big deal—the last year of elementary school. We were the oldest students at Academy, and I was anticipating the new responsibilities we were expected to handle. As sixth graders, we would help run the school store at lunchtime, selling Hershey bars and pencils to younger students. We would also operate the school traffic patrol to make sure everyone safely crossed the busy intersection of Kanawha Street and College Avenue. This year, we would even get a chance to give parents tours of the new section of the school building.

Walking through the big red front door, I discovered I would be in Mrs. Hicks' classroom. Remembering that Mrs. Hicks was taller than my father and hearing her booming voice, I nervously entered my new room. As I spotted old friends—Chris, Pam,

Bunny, Cathy, Nick, Benny—I started to feel right at home.

All of a sudden, that big tease Joe yelled out to me, "Hey. There's the Jolly Green Giant." Unfortunately, it looked like I would be stuck with my dreaded nickname for another year—just because I was the tallest kid in the class again. I had really hoped Donna would catch up with me during the summer. I laughed with Joe and tried to remember what Mom always told me, "Stand straight, Annie. The boys will catch up to you some day."

Besides, I was already thinking about more important things. Would hot lunch in the basement cafeteria taste any better or would the mac and cheese still clump together? Maybe I'd have to bring my bologna sandwich another year. Would the old bathroom still look so dark and frightening now that I was a year older? What would it feel like to switch classes to Mr. Mearns for math and reading? Would Academy have another Spelling Bee? I was nervous during the county level contest last year, but Dad and Mom were proud of me being the best speller in my school. Do I really want to spend my evenings practicing lists of words when I'd rather talk with my friends on the telephone?

With all those thoughts swirling around in my head, I finally settled down at my little wooden desk, put my pencil in the groove on top, got out a clean sheet of paper, and started my sixth-grade year.

MY BRIER
Anne

"Here Brier! Here Brier!"

This call, along with a loud whistle, was a familiar sound in the Almond household. We always had a collie dog named Brier. Or should I say, Dad always had a dog that he graciously "assigned" to one of us: Greenbrier's Brier, K's Brier, Anne's Brier (Ruth's dog was named Licker because we had two dogs at once) and Beth's McBrier.

I remember my Brier the best because he was the dog we had during those growing-up years from preschool through seventh grade. He was our constant and closest companion. Each of us loved him as our friend, and before the days of leash laws and fences, we took Brier everywhere we went. He barked with glee as we made angels in the new-fallen snow. He helped us run through the sprinkler on hot summer days. He cuddled up with us by the fireplace and slept at the foot of our beds. Mom encouraged him to go with us on hikes through the fields because he "chased the snakes away." She was not happy, though, when this same sweet dog ruined her flowers by plopping on top of her gladiolus and geraniums. Nonetheless, Brier and Mom shared a special relationship, keeping each other company when his playmates—and her kids—were at school each day.

Brier watched over us and provided company and comfort. One afternoon when I was only four, I was running my fastest to keep up with the older kids in the neighborhood gang as they raced down the road in front of the Daniels' house. Scurrying on my short, chubby legs, I tripped on the coal-based road and skinned my knee pretty badly. The other kids, not hearing my yells, ran on ahead, but Brier returned to me immediately. He stood perfectly still beside me, letting me grab his long hair to pull myself up. With sniffles and a bloody knee, I hobbled home, holding tight to my dog's collar.

When I was more grown up, around age ten, and needed to escape the chaos of our noisy house, Brier and I would often walk to the pine thickets of the City Park to our secret "thinking spot." Brier would plop down and I'd spread out on the cool ground beside him, resting my head on his soft belly. Nothing was more comforting than lying there with him, looking at the blue sky peeping through the trees.

While Brier made each one of us feel like his favorite, he liked everyone. He loved greeting houseguests and hanging out on second base when we played neighborhood softball and gently putting his nose on Mrs. Stansberry's lap and nudging Grandma Flanagan. He nipped at our horse Pinto Scout and teased the cat Dick Ralston and chased our rabbits Pete and RePeat.

Brier's appearance in several Christmas pictures is a testimony to his status as a valued member of our family—Brier posing on the living room couch, Brier by the fence, Brier in front of the swing under the maple tree. He was happiest playing with his kids, barking at our heels as we ran through the fields or sledded down the snowy hills.

The summer I was twelve, Brier lost his long battle with epilepsy. Mom walked out to the horse pasture where I was camping with friends. She stuck her head into our tent and told me that my Brier was dying. As I stepped onto the back porch, he tried to lift his head and managed a small thump of his tail. I sprawled out next to him one last time, gave him a big hug, and bid farewell to my good friend.

EASTER
Ruthie

Every spring we got new outfits for Easter. I remember one year getting a new spring dress with matching yellow, patent leather shoes. We attended church as a family every Sunday. And on Easter we got to wear our new outfits to church.

We had many other Easter traditions as a family as well. On the Saturday evening before Easter, we five siblings dyed eggs that Mom had first hard cooked. This was an activity that Dad always seemed to enjoy as well. We filled older coffee cups with hot water, vinegar, and a dye tablet from the kits Daddy had gotten for us. The kits had wax crayons for drawing on the eggs before dipping them in the warm, purple, blue, or green smelly liquid. We took the eggs out with a little wire hook and let them drip-dry on the newspaper-covered kitchen table.

After the egg dying time, we children got out our individual Easter baskets, which were saved from year to year, just like our Christmas stockings were. We filled our baskets with fake green or yellow grass and then left them out for the Easter Bunny. After we went to bed, Mom would hide them either in the kitchen or the living room.

On Easter morning we hunted for our baskets. One year we couldn't find one until Mom got up. She knew the Bunny had put that one inside the stereo speaker. The baskets had lots of jellybeans, chocolate cream-filled eggs, a chocolate rabbit, and some of our colored eggs from the night before. We each took some of our jellybeans and filled a large cardboard egg for Mom and Dad. After finding our baskets, eating breakfast, and dressing in our new outfits, we went off to church. Afterward, we had dinner back at home. Then came the next big event.

Buckhannon's city park, next to our home, was turned into an Easter egg hunt for the community. Children lined up by ages, and each age group was given a place to hunt for as many Easter eggs as possible. The plastic eggs contained candies, and prizes were given to those who collected the most eggs.

Easter always seemed like a fun time with spring colors and newness of the first crocuses and daffodils that bloomed in the March or April gardens. They were the same colors as our eggs!

OPEN BOOK
Ruthie

When I was in fifth grade, my birthday present that year was a hardcover copy of the biography of George Washington Carver. It was rare to have a hardcover book of my own. We borrowed many books from the school and local libraries. Our home was filled with books for young children that Mom read and reread to all of us five children.

We had paperback books that were purchased from school fundraisers. My older siblings had several books from a series entitled *We Were There*. But now I had my very own hardcover book about a famous American.

I read with wonder the life of that famous Southern African-American man. Carver had a strong desire to learn. He went on to develop multiple uses for the peanut. I remember how hardworking, inventive, and oh-so-smart the man in my book was.

That book influenced me well into college. I came from a town with five black families and went off to a college where 15% of the students were African American. The cultural shock that could have been a bit daunting for me was cushioned by the book I had read in fifth grade, as well as copies of *Ebony* magazine delivered regularly to our home. My freshman roommate was black. While in college I took a black history course and a black literature course. I dated black men.

That book influenced my open attitude.

4-H CAMP
Ruthie

I am glad I went to 4-H camp each summer, since 4-H club and its projects were a large part of my childhood life. However, at the time and even looking back, there were pros and cons about going to and being at 4-H camp.

The drive to Selbyville in the southern end of our Upshur County was long and curvy. I had to pack whatever I thought I would need for all five days, leaving behind at home my mom, my cats, and my privacy.

Camp life was run on a schedule for all 24 hours each day. A bell to get up, a bell to line up for meals, classes in the morning and sports in the afternoon, supper in the evening, and the big campfire each evening.

At camp, we were always part of a "tribe." There were four tribes, and I was a Mingo. My older sister Anne had been a Mingo, too. I probably couldn't pick K's Cherokees or Greenbrier's Delaware, since in tribe cheers we had to spell out the name of our tribe, and I never could spell.

After the evening campfire, we had a little time to get to our cabins and wash up. Then it was lights out and quiet at the sound of another bell. Each tribe was rewarded or penalized for each member's performance or obedience. Was our lunch line straight? Mingos would get four points. Was my bed maintained perfectly? A point for our tribe. Did we win the volleyball game? More points. Did the counselors like our cheer or skit or story around the campfire? We got points. At the end of the week, one tribe won first place.

Perhaps it was a good lesson to learn to come in third place. I did not like the wet dew and early mornings. I did like the sunset and the echo over the hills. The river, the wide valley, the grassy yard, and the athletic playing fields were serene settings. The food was always good, even if the cement dining hall was noisy. Several of my town friends came with me to 4-H camp.

By the time I reached junior-high and high school, I knew most of the other 4-H-ers, no matter where they were from. Our West Virginia in the 1950s and 1960s didn't have much diversity, except an imaginary one between city and country. We also had few children with disabilities. One gal, Nancy, with muscular dystrophy, who used a crutch to walk, was a 4-H-er. She was also a Mingo. Children often struggle with someone who is different. I am thankful today I knew Nancy during those summer camp days, since we have renewed our friendship in the last dozen years. Nancy, who is near my age, presently lives in a nursing home. She is a brave woman, whom I enjoy visiting whenever I return to my hometown. 4-H camp offered me that opportunity.

Another positive outcome from those camp years is being able to look back at my parents' commitment to 4-H and Selbyville. Dad was the camp doctor. He checked all the children for general health on the first day of camp. He returned to camp for any health needs. He also loved to visit camp for a meal. Mom often joined him, during the week, usually on Thursday evening.

Mom wrote her children a postcard or two during our five days at camp. Those five days seemed so long. My parents worked for years to have a swimming pool built at the camp, since the river swimming hole seemed a bit dangerous to Dad. The experience of trying to raise the money to build the pool made my parents compassionate and understanding toward me years later, when I had to begin to raise all my funds to be a full-time missionary. They knew that expectations from some folks could be brought low, and yet the most unlikely person would make a sacrificial gift.

The pool finally got built at the camp. It is probably one of the reasons that camp has continued to be used by hundreds of youth who not only attend 4-H camp there, but also church youth camp and band camp. They too can wake up in the morning and hear the whippoorwills.

A SECURE PLACE
Ruthie

What was my favorite place in my childhood home? Our two-story red-brick house with a full basement on three acres of land was an ideal place for our family to grow and to welcome others. I loved the warmth and welcome that my mother extended to all who came through the entrance.

I know the physical parts of our big house because over the years I had chores to do or I could earn some spending money by cleaning various surfaces. I dry-mopped the hardwood floors, and wet-mopped the kitchen and porch floors. I washed all the windows. I shellacked the more than two-dozen wooden French-style casement windows one summer. One year, I cleaned the bathrooms weekly. I fixed loose screws or hung picture frames whenever needed.

I loved my bedroom in that house. Beth, who shared the large room for many years with me, and I could look out on the front to see who was coming, or out the two back windows that overlooked a distant downtown Buckhannon or our Christmas-tree pines in the back side yard.

We had three closets in that room. In the back of one of the two clothes closets was also a hidden closet. The short, wooden, hidden door led to a slanted, strange area. The third closet in our room was also under the eaves, with a door that led into a child-sized play area. This is where we kept our toys. With Beth or a girl friend or a neighbor girl, I would play for hours with my Barbie and Ken dolls. These were Barbie's very early days.

Looking back in surprise, I realize that I got some of my first feminist ideas from that doll couple. Barbie had her own car and her own dream house. She made many of the decisions about her career and her relationship activities with Ken.

In that play closet, I would imagine and roleplay. It was a secure place to have intimate little-girl conversations.

Later in my youth, that closet was the place to have a small bookshelf and to keep treasures from childhood. My parents let me keep that closet well into adulthood. Only recently, in my late middle-age years, have I moved all my physical belongings out of that magical room in that special house. However, the sweetest memories and love of the atmosphere of my childhood home, my room, and my closet are still warm in my heart.

HE FELL OUT OF BED
AND CHANGED OUR LIVES
Beth

It was late autumn and the frost was thick the night the phone call came that would change my life. And as these matters of fate so often unravel, I had yet to be born. Not many people back in the 1950s had two telephones in their house, but the extra one was in the master bedroom, situated on the lower shelf of the built-in bookshelves, several steps from the bed, so the doctor would have to stand and truly wake up when he said his sleep-graveled hello. It was a rare night when there wasn't a call in the middle of the night.

"Doc, could you please come to Hemlock right away? My husband's fallen out of bed and I'm afraid he's broken his hip. He's just in awful pain and can't hardly move. I'm going to put my neighbor on the telephone and she'll tell you how to get to the house—I need to get back home to him."

The doctor closed his eyes and listened carefully as the neighbor gave directions, only interrupting once, "She's in her 80s and she walked over a mile through the wilderness to get to your house, with only a lantern to light her way?" He hung up and gently whispered to his wife that he probably wouldn't be back until daybreak, he and Brier were headed to Hemlock, 22 miles away, the last half on roads barely wide enough for a school bus. He grabbed his black bag from the kitchen table where he had been rubbing it with saddle soap the evening before, checked inside it for morphine and a syringe, and headed out into the Milky Way clear darkness. The collie dog was ready and waiting by the door.

"Ah, Brier, Hemlock, West Virginia—the site of one of the seven wonders of Upshur County, Upshur Mountain, the highest point in the county, over 3,000 feet. We're going to be riding up a few ridges tonight, might even see some snow." The dog and the man rode in companionable silence as they headed through Tallmansville, past the turn-off to Ten Mile and Sago, over the bridges at Lower and then Upper Queens, and began the steep ascent up the narrow passage on Taylor Hill to Hemlock Ridge. The road became dirt, the houses fewer, and the quarter moon as silvery as the foxes curled up in their nearby dens. At the fork in the road, the left turn heading to the one-room schoolhouse and the Methodist church, the doctor took the hairpin curve to the right, leading to the combination country store and post office, keeping his eye out for a "lane you might miss, Doc, and if you get to the wooden bridge, turn around and go back a piece and you'll see it."

The old man and woman didn't have a car and the road was a path, the doctor's old Army Jeep bouncing through mud holes, scraping on branches, and running perilously close to the steep bank of the creek, a tributary to the Middle Fork River. As he came around the last curve and up the rise to the meadow, the doctor stopped as the cabin came into view—wide logs, a tall chimney of huge rocks, two towering Hemlock trees alongside, planted, no doubt, on the day the couple was married and moved into their home.

Though writhing in pain, the old gentleman did not have a fracture, and after the doctor lifted him into bed with his strong arms and administered a shot of morphine, the man smiled and fell asleep. "Doc, I want to show you something," the old woman said. She took up the lantern by the door and led him across the field to a trail running alongside the river. They wove in and out of the trees, through thick moss, under rhododendron and mountain laurel branches, stepped over an old corduroy logging road, and came out onto a huge rock in the river where the waterfalls filled the quiet of the frosty pre-dawn. He turned to the woman and said, "Ma'am, you live in Paradise."

The doctor and dog were quiet on the ride back home. His wife was making a pot of coffee and he went over and gave her a kiss. "Lois, I've never coveted anything before, but I am in awe right now. I've seen the place of my dreams and I hope we can have it someday. It would be the greatest gift we could ever give the children."

It was a number of years after that nighttime house call, after the deaths of the old man and woman—and the passing of the doctor's own father, leaving him a simple inheritance, the exact amount needed to buy that hundred acres of heaven—that my father's prophetic wisdom came true. It was the greatest gift to his children, grandchildren, great-grandchildren. No matter where we roam over this vast planet, and we do seem to be wanderers, each of us knows there is a spot in the mountains of West Virginia that calls out to us, cradles our spirits, and holds precious memories of first loves, camping trips, digging ramps, driving lessons, horseshoe games, tree houses, dam building, fire circles, hiking, wildflowers, soothing tears—and giggles over how our Tom Sawyer parents invented the "wish being granted on the third rock thrown into the big mud hole," which hole, of course, no longer exists. (I swear to this day that third rock wish is how I got my first husband.) And the waterfalls has become the Mecca one conjures up while in the dentist chair or caught by stopped traffic in the city—the mere image brings a smile, a sigh, and memories of holes worn in the seats of our pants as we mentally slide down the falls into the cold, clear mountain stream.

MOTHERS OF BUCKHANNON
Beth

Back in 1907, Miss Anna Jarvis, a woman who was never to become a mother herself, held the first Mother's Day service as a memorial to her mother, in Grafton, West Virginia. Decades later, she announced to the world that she wished she'd never started the tradition. What began as an honoring of mothers became a commercial holiday and this saddened her. But the holiday became popular and continues to be celebrated throughout the world. Frankly, I'm glad. Though it brings a pain to the heart as I reach for a white carnation instead of a red one at the door of our beautiful rock church along the Blue Ridge Parkway, the memory of my own mother is clearly one to celebrate. And there is the recollection of so many women who touched my life in a motherly way as I grew up in a small town in central West Virginia.

My mother, Lois Ruth, was a kind and gentle soul, as well as strong in so many ways. When I am asked to describe her, I often say three things: a Methodist, a botanist, a 4-H'er. Her creed in life could be summed up in one sentence, if one can actually do that for someone as personal as a mother. I will try: My mother hated alcohol, thought God cried when the mountains were stripped for coal, and the trilliums and topsoil and bubbling creeks were pushed asunder, and was always pushing herself and her children to "make the best better."

There were so many strong and resourceful women in our little town of Buckhannon. My earliest memories of Saturday night family gatherings bring to mind Ella Berisford, Irma St. Clair, Hazel Beer. Aren't those wonderful names? Ella, Irma, Hazel—names from another era; ladies who loved their children and spread that love to their friends' children, too.

And the neighborhood mothers of Victoria Hill. They kept their eyes on all of us, but in an independent way that encouraged our all-day hikes and building of forts and softball games and tree house construction. Knowing when to bring out the watermelons and gather all the gang around first one house and the next week another. I salute them—Alice Williams, Rose Lockwood, Lena Stansberry, Martha Daniel, Splash Williams,

Mona Oldaker, Vivian Shaffer, Sarah Chamberlain, Jo Morgan, and Martha Shissler. They made childhood sweet.

Those first few years of school, our teachers were often like mothers to us. Helen Reger was an angel on this earth. Martha Jane Phillips gave me a lifelong love of reading. Olive Baxa can still make me smile when I think of her laugh. Katherine Steur had the prettiest sweaters I had ever seen. Delma Iden read us *Charlie and the Chocolate Factory* and is the only teacher for whom I earned straight *A*'s. She had a marvelous way of bringing out the best in her students, even in my handwriting, which often left much to be desired. I thank Edith Hall in my mind every time I have to multiply numbers. Mary Rinard had the patience of a saint. Betty Hicks taught me respect for myself. And Hope Butterfield was a teacher who let us come to her house on a Saturday and become her friend. But she also made me sing the only solo I have ever sung in my life.

As time went on, my best friends' mothers rose to the occasion and reached out to us at those moments when we needed someone other than our own mothers. There were the mothers who were actually fun and would take us shopping and join in our card games and show a real interest in our boy worries and other angsts: Peg Clark, Jane Reddecliff, Sue Martin, Susie Miller, Pat Turner. And those who would talk to us with respect, like Bunny Mow and Anna Thompson. And mothers who treated us with politeness and interest and concern: Betty Allman and Virginia Hunnicutt. And then there was Maxine Hinkle, who let us take over her house on Saturday afternoons so a gang of us could laugh and dance and make bologna and potato chip sandwiches and just be girls. And I could salute more, but as the decades have passed, the memories and the names become fuzzier, but remain warm.

My last salute is to my godmother, Beth Darnell, a woman with natural class and grace, who lived in what I thought of as the grandest house in town, a columned home, shaded with maples, on Meade Street. We shared a name and a friendship between a young girl and an older woman. She gave me gifts each year on my birthday and Christmas. It would be her gift I asked for each Christmas Eve when we returned home from church and Mother would let us open one gift before bed. I always knew it would be something I would cherish. To this day, I sometimes reach far into my jewelry box and pull out the sterling silver figure of a young woman, engraved with the name of Beth. I hold it close and conjure up the times of childhood. A time when there were so many mothers in my life.

UNITED NATIONS ON THE HILL
Beth

My mom, upon receiving the alumni award from West Virginia Wesleyan College, was described as the "Mother to the Nations," honoring her hosting of 99 different folks from a variety of countries over the years. Some guests would come for a few days over holiday breaks or for the summer months—and then there was dear Friday, the Nigerian student who came for a semester and stayed four years. He was a hard worker who mowed the grass and wiped down the shower. The perfect child.

Being a rather ardent feminist in my late teen years, I had my work cut out convincing Friday there was no such thing as "women's work" when it came to washing and drying dishes or sweeping the kitchen floor. His father had four wives back in Africa, and Friday would chuckle and shake his head as he stood with a towel drying the dishes. "Oh, Beth, they would laugh at me back home. My, how they would laugh!"

Friday's perfect balance was exemplary. He would often stride down the street with his briefcase on his head, paying no attention to gawking strangers who, no doubt, told themselves: "… must be another of the Almond's visitors …" Central West Virginia did not see many folks of color or different nationalities back in those days.

Friday was an exceptional tennis player, another rarity in our part of the state. There were few tennis players of Friday's rank and ability. It just happened that two such Buckhannon men would call the house, setting up games with Friday. One was a local businessman who had his own tennis court. The other was a fellow who rang up, stating, "This is Jay, calling for Friday." To everyone else, Jay was known as the president of the local college. A few years after the fast and exciting tennis games with Friday, Jay went on to become our West Virginia governor and then U. S. Senator John D. Rockefeller, IV.

Our house often took on the roll of a mini United Nations. Mom was the West Virginia hostess for the Experiment in International Living, a program where teachers, university students, professionals of all types, would come and live with American families. One time, in the midst of a major international blow-up between Turkey and Cyprus, we had guests over the Christmas holiday—two Turks and a Cypriot. George, a Duke University student from Cyprus who had stayed with us over the summer, could not afford the airfare home for vacation. The Turks, both agricultural professionals, were taking several weeks to learn more about American life. The three men glared around our kitchen, mumbling under their breaths, "No good Turk but a dead Turk." "No good Cypriot but a dead one." We were faced with a diplomatic dilemma. Laws! My mom hated conflict of any kind, and she was also not one to give up easily. She took George aside and asked him for some patience. I took the Turks out to a local dairy for a private tour, sweetening the afternoon with homemade ice cream from the dairy's shop.

    Slowly, over days of singing Christmas carols and eating meals together, the men began to chat, exchanging stories from their lives. My lasting memory of that holiday, when I was no more than 16 or 17 years old, is a picture in my mind of those three fellows rolling out cookie dough on the big kitchen table, laughter and lightness in the room, a fire crackling in the fireplace and spreading a radiant warmth—and the hugs given to each other and to their American Mom. "Lord, make me an instrument of your peace."

ALSO AVAILABLE

The Stories of a West Virginia Doctor
 Harold D. Almond, MD

Tender Loving Care: Stories of a West Virginia Doctor, Volume II
 Stories of Harold Almond, MD as told to
 Greenbrier Almond, MD

Stories of a West Virginia Doctor's Son
 Greenbrier Almond, MD

Stories of a West Virginia Doctor for His Grandchildren
 Greenbrier Almond, MD

Stories of a West Virginia Doctor for Kith and Kin
 Greenbrier Almond, MD

Available from:
    Artistry on Main
    27 E. Main St. Buckhannon, WV 26201

    Upshur County Historical Society
    29 W. Main St. Buckhannon, WV 26201
    www.upshurcountyhistoricalsociety.com

    McClain Printing Company
    1-800-654-7179 www.mcclainprinting.com

    West Virginia Book Company
    1-888-982-7472 www.wvbookco.com

    Amazon.com

    Barnesandnoble.com

    Gift shops throughout the state, including
    Stonewall Resort, St. Joseph's Hospital, Tamarack